READING COMPREHENSION

New Directions for Classroom Practice

READING COMPREHENSION

New Directions for Classroom Practice

John D. McNeil

University of California, Los Angeles

Scott, Foresman and Company

Glenview, Illinois
London, England

Library of Congress Cataloging in Publication Data

McNeil, John D.
  Reading comprehension.

  Includes bibliographies and index.
  1. Reading comprehension. I. Title.
LB1050.45.M38   1984   372.4′1   84-1396
ISBN 0-673-15835-7

3 4 5 6 7 - EBI - 89 88 87 86 85 84

ACKNOWLEDGMENTS

(p. 6) From PHI DELTA KAPPAN, Vol. 64, No. 1, September 1982. Copyright © 1982 Martha F. Campbell. Reprinted by permission of the Phi Delta Kappan.

(p. 15) From ECT 401 Classroom Processes—Task, Pupil, and Teacher, pp. 48, 50–53. Deakin University Open Campus Program. Copyright © 1981 Deakin University, Victoria, Australia.

(p. 15) Reprinted by permission of Scholastic Inc. from AESOP'S FABLES retold by Ann McGovern. Copyright © 1963 by Scholastic Inc.

(p. 28) From "Active Comprehension" by Harry Singer, READING TEACHER, May 1978. Copyright © 1978 International Reading Association. Reprinted with permission of Harry Singer and the International Reading Association.

(p. 35) From "Using the Experience Text Relationship Method with Minority Children" by Kathryn Au, READING TEACHER, March 1977. Copyright © 1977 International Reading Association. Reprinted with permission of Kathryn Au and the International Reading Association.

(p. 45) From MIND'S EYE. Escondido School District, Escondido, CA, Board of Education, 1979. Reprinted by permission.

(p. 64) Table 4–1 from ACCRETION, TUNING, RESTRUCTURING: THREE MODES OF LEARNING by David Rumelhart and Donald Norman, Report 7602, La Jolla Center for Human Information Processing, August 1976. Reprinted by permission.

(p. 66) From HUNGER OF MEMORY: THE EDUCATION OF RICHARD RODRIGUEZ by Richard Rodriguez. Copyright © 1981 by Richard Rodriguez. Reprinted by permission of David R. Godine, Publisher, Boston.

(p. 70) From "Alternative Frameworks: Conceptual conflict and accommodation: Toward a principled teaching strategy" by J. Nussbaum and S. Novick in INSTRUCTIONAL SCIENCE, Vol. 11, 1982. Reprinted by permission of Elsevier Science Publishers.

(p. 85) From THE PRODUCTIVE THINKING PROGRAM by Martin V. Covington, Lillian Davies, Richard S. Crutchfield, and Robert M. Ofton, Jr. Reprinted by permission of Charles Merrill Publishing Co.

(p. 88) From TEACHING READING COMPREHENSION by P. David Pearson and Dale D. Johnson. Copyright © 1978. Reprinted by permission of Holt, Rinehart and Winston.

(p. 90) From "Question-Answering Strategies for Children" by Taffy E. Raphael, READING TEACHER, November 1982. Copyright © 1982 International Reading Association. Reprinted with permission of Taffy E. Raphael and the International Reading Association.

(p. 102) From A REVIEW OF TRENDS IN VOCABULARY RESEARCH AND THE EFFECTS OF PRIOR KNOWLEDGE ON INSTRUCTIONAL STRATEGIES FOR VOCABULARY ACQUISITION by Dale D. Johnson, Susan Toms-Bronowski, and Susan D. Pittelman. Wisconsin Center for Education Research, University of Wisconsin, November 1981. Reprinted by permission of Dale D. Johnson.

Preface

Only a few years ago the teaching of reading was concerned with the problem of going from symbols to sound and from written words to spoken words. Little attention was given to the process of comprehending the meaning of text. For example, in 1979, Dolores Durkin completed a study involving classroom observations of the teaching of reading comprehension at the request of the National Institute of Education.[1] Grades 3–6 were the focus for these observations on the ground that more comprehension instruction would be found at these grade levels than in the primary grades. To everyone's surprise, Durkin found practically *no* comprehension instruction. There was only comprehension *assessment* and concern about whether children's answers were right or wrong. Assignments categorized as *comprehension* consisted chiefly of answering questions; matching partial sentences on one side of a workbook page with partial sentences listed on the other side; arranging sentences in sequential order; matching items; and explaining the meaning of idiomatic expressions.

Now the priorities have shifted—reading for meaning is of first importance. Teachers are teaching reading comprehension, and their students are learning to comprehend text. Both teachers and researchers have become more knowledgeable about the complexities of written comprehension. Serious scholars from such diverse disciplines as cognitive psychology, artificial intelligence, linguistics, and reading education have contributed to our understanding of the reading process, and teachers have begun to validate the new theory and research in their classroom practices. No longer do teachers need lament the lack of appropriate knowledge and methods for teaching reading comprehension.

Reading Comprehension: New Directions for Classroom Practice brings together in a practical way the strategies and materials suggested by recent developments in the study of reading comprehension. The book is intended for use in undergraduate and graduate courses in reading methods. Teachers will find it valuable in their work with children and adults alike. Scholars concerned with the reading process will find the book useful for the way it demonstrates how both theory and empirical findings can inform practice.

Although the work samples widely from the different disciplines, there is coherence both in the focus upon reading comprehension and a unifying assumption about reading as an interactive process between reader and text by which meaning is both found and created.

Each chapter includes the background and rationale for the practices described. Ways for teachers to determine the accuracy of the major

[1] Dolores Durkin, "What Classroom Observations Reveal About Reading Comprehension Instruction," *Reading Research Quarterly* 4, 14 (1978–79): 481–533.

hypotheses and the potential teaching strategies are given in each chapter. The book has a concluding summary or Coda to help one integrate the ideas presented. Some readers may prefer to begin with the Coda, using it as an advanced organizer to the text.

Chapters One, Two, and Three contain much of the constructivist theory which is so important in understanding newer teaching and learning strategies. The emphasis in these chapters is upon *assimilation* in reading, the linking of prior experiences to new information and knowledge.

Chapter Four emphasizes *accommodation,* the modification of those preconceptions or "alternate frameworks" that keep one from acquiring and using new knowledge from text.

Chapter Five illustrates how studies of metacognition relate to teaching students how to learn more effectively as independent readers. Self-knowledge, awareness of the reading tasks, and ways to guide students in processing written information are among the important features.

In Chapters Six, Seven, and Eight, there are opportunities to acquire new strategies for old tasks—vocabulary development, following the structure of a passage, identifying a writer's technique and formulating the main thought of a passage.

Reading Comprehension: New Directions for Classroom Practice can be read as an informative piece about new developments in reading comprehension. Each chapter begins with a review of current theory and related research. It can be read for its suggestions for both *what* and *how* to teach for better comprehension. There are model lessons showing how to implement the strategies. Finally, the book can be read as a guide to inquiry. The activities within each chapter offer opportunities to validate the strategies with colleagues in a study group or in one's own classroom, trying out the new strategies.

I wish to acknowledge my debt to Mary Ellen McNeil for her intellectual and professional support during the preparation of the manuscript. Also, I appreciate the helpful suggestions made by the reviewers: Yetta Goodman, Claire Weinstein, Tom Trabasso, Victoria Chou Hare, and Beau Jones. The editorial assistance of Anita Portugal was outstanding, contributing to a much improved text. Finally, I wish to thank Christopher Jennison of the Scott, Foresman Professional Publishing Group, whose vision, guidance, and encouragement made the book possible.

John D. McNeil

Contents

READING COMPREHENSION
New Directions for Classroom Practice

1 Reading Comprehension as a Cognitive Process: The Assessment of Schemata for Reading

COMPREHENSION AS PROCESS

WHAT TESTS TELL US ABOUT READING COMPREHENSION

SCHEMA THEORY

APPLYING SCHEMA THEORY IN BUILDING AND ACTIVATING PUPILS' BACKGROUND KNOWLEDGE
Constructing a Semantic Map

APPLYING SCHEMA THEORY IN ASSESSING PUPILS' COMPREHENSION OF STORIES

APPLYING SCHEMA THEORY IN ASSESSING PUPILS' CONCEPTS OF READING

SUMMARY

Overview

This chapter looks at reading comprehension as an interaction between reader and text by which meaning is created. It stresses the importance of helping pupils acquire the process for creating meaning and introduces schema theory—a key to newer interpretation of reading comprehension. What is schema theory? What does it have to do with teaching? How can a teacher apply schema theory in activating background knowledge and assessing comprehension? How can the teacher determine the pupil's schema for reading, and how do different schemata for reading affect comprehension? Chapter 1 answers these questions.

COMPREHENSION AS PROCESS

At one time little effort was made to teach the process of reading comprehension. Early analyses of reading seemed to assume that once readers could decode accurately and fluently, comprehension would automatically follow. Even when this assumption was found to be false, efforts to improve comprehension focused more on product than on process. Pupils were asked to answer questions about directly stated facts and to infer answers from written material without considering how to achieve such understanding. A vocabulary pertinent to a given selection might be taught, but the learner was rarely taught how to comprehend the text in general. Because pupils were given feedback on the accuracy of their performance in answering questions, the instruction was more comprehension practice with delayed feedback than instruction in how to comprehend.

In contrast with the older emphasis on teaching reading comprehension as *product* by asking pupils to answer questions about their reading, newer approaches stress teaching reading comprehension as *process*. Accordingly, pupils are taught techniques for processing text—making inferences, activating appropriate concepts, relating new information to old, creating picture images, and reducing the information in a text to a main idea.

Four assumptions underlying the process approach are:

1. *What pupils already know affects what they will learn from reading.* The reader's prior knowledge interacts with text to create psychological meaning. Background knowledge determines the interpretations made from text. Researchers refer to prior knowledge as knowledge structure, scripts, frames, or schemata (plural for *schema*). Schemata are frameworks for interrelating different elements of information about a topic. Comprehending a message involves constructing a correspondence between an existing schema and the elements in the message. That is, the schema is a framework of expectations. It allows the reader to take what is directly perceivable and to make inferences about its unseen features. By way of example, try to comprehend the following sentence suggested by Bransford and McCarrell without using schema.

   The notes were sour because the seams split.

   Although the syntax is simple and the individual words are easy, the sentence does not make sense to most people. However, it does become meaningful as soon as one hears the word *bagpipe,* which fits into a schema containing slots for associated objects (pipes, pipers), actions (playing a musical instrument, marching), and qualities (musical).[1]

Teachers will regard the researcher's emphasis upon the role of background knowledge as consistent with their traditional practices of preteaching vocabulary and providing requisite background experiences. Other newer techniques for activating background knowledge—semantic mapping and student-generated questions—are also relevant.

2. *Both concept-driven and data-driven processes are necessary in comprehending text.* A concept-driven process calls for activating schemata and applying them in setting expectations for reading and for filling gaps in one's schemata with information read in the text.

A concept-driven process is a "top-down" strategy in which the reader's goals and expectations determine what is read. In contrast, data-driven processing occurs when the reader attends to the text and then searches for structures (schemata) in which to fit the incoming information. The reader monitors information from the bottom-up, replacing initial expectations with new ones triggered by the text. Different words and sentences suggest new expectations.

Good readers approach texts with top-down strategy and then use selected schemata to integrate the text, discarding schemata that are inappropriate. Less able readers tend to overrely on either a top-down strategy or a text-driven process, which has a deleterious effect on comprehension. An overemphasis on top-down processing results in inferences that are not warranted by the text, while an overemphasis on bottom-up processing—staying close to print—results in word calling.

3. *The deeper a person processes text, the more he or she will remember and understand it.* The deep-processing thesis rests on two strategies for understanding text—elaboration and the use of the author's organizational framework. Elaboration is an embellishment of text; readers accomplish it by drawing upon their prior knowledge, making inferences, paraphrasing the text in their own language, and relating it to their own purposes.

As an example of elaboration and its effects, consider a study in which less successful fifth-grade pupils received training in how to produce precise elaborations and as a result showed a large increase in their retention of what they read.[2] Pupils were first made aware of

---

[1] J. D. Bransford and N. S. McCarrell, "A Sketch of a Cognitive Approach to Comprehension," in *Cognition and the Symbolic Process*, ed. W. B. Weiner and D. Palmero (Hillsdale, N.J.: Erlbaum, 1974).

[2] B. Stein et al. "Differences in the Precision of Self-Generated Elaborations," *Journal of Experimental Psychology* 3 (1982): 399–405.

sentences that were difficult to remember or difficult to learn. Next, they learned to differentiate precise from imprecise elaborations. Precise elaboration clarifies the significance or relevance of a stated fact. Thus, for the sentence *The hungry man got into his car,* the elaboration *to go to the restaurant* would be precise (relevant), while the elaboration *and drove away* would not be. Pupils were prompted to activate knowledge that would make the relationships between a statement and its elaboration less arbitrary and to spontaneously ask themselves how their elaborations related to the statements.

Deep processing using the author's framework requires that the reader identify the patterns by which the text is organized—narratives, for example, are most often organized by general structures, such as setting, characterization, theme, key episode, and resolution of a problem that motivated the character to take action. Expository texts are usually organized by use of certain patterns for ordering statements—presenting facts and details in relation to more general and important statements, for example. Readers process more deeply when reading narratives by relating specific events and details to the general structure. Similarly, when reading expository selections, readers achieve deeper processing when they find the connections among supporting details, examples, main ideas, and high-level abstractions.

4. *The context in which reading occurs influences what will be recalled.* An example that supports this generalization is found in a study by Anderson and Pichert.[3] The investigators demonstrated that students interpreted passages differently when given different perspectives— those of a homebuyer and a burglar. The "homebuyers" learned and remembered information relevant to the problems of living in a home. The "burglars" learned and remembered information related to security, such as the location of doors, lights, and windows. Apparently the perspective activated particular schemata.

Prior knowledge and attitude constitute major contexts for comprehending. Wrestlers' and music majors' recall after reading the same text, for example, was found to evidence the selectivity patterns of each group's prior knowledge and interest.[4] Individuals with a strong stand on a particular issue (ego-involved individuals) will interpret statements about that issue differently from those without a stand.

In brief, reading comprehension as process involves actively constructing meaning among the parts of the text and between the

---

[3] R. C. Anderson and J. W. Pichert, "Recall of Previously Unrecallable Information Following a Shift in Perspective," *Journal of Verbal Learning and Verbal Behavior* 17 (1978): 1–12.
[4] R. C. Anderson, R. E. Reynolds, D. C. Schallert, and E. T. Goetz, "Frameworks for Comprehending Discourse," *American Education Journal* 14 (1977): 357–82.

text and personal experience. The text itself is but a blueprint for the creating of meaning. Comprehension and retention are enhanced by strategies for relating text with personal knowledge and experience.

WHAT TESTS TELL US ABOUT READING COMPREHENSION

Numerous reasons have been given for failure to perform well on tests of reading comprehension—failure to decode words, inability to follow directions, inability to explain or remember, insufficient vocabulary, lack of interest in the material, complexity of syntax, and complexity of ideas and their relations.

However, sometimes failure to do well on a test is the fault of the test. Tests that are labeled tests of comprehension often measure something else. Standardized tests, for example, are often developed according to a procedure whereby the items that everybody gets right are discarded, although these items might represent important aspects of reading comprehension; conversely, items retained might not be valid measures of comprehension.

"I knew the answers. I just couldn't retrieve them from my memory bank."

Most tests of reading comprehension follow an outline of skills suggested by Fred Davis as comprehension skills that can be measured objectively.[5] These skills are knowing word meaning, reasoning, concentrating on the literal sense of meaning, following the structure of a passage, and recognizing the mood and literary techniques of a writer. Tests measuring these skills have been criticized because they give a limited view of what comprises reading; the tasks required by the tests inadequately represent the wide range and level of possible reading tasks, and the questions examine only a proportion of what could be comprehended in the text.[6] Such tests are not very useful in helping a teacher understand the pupil's processes of reading comprehension, because the teacher cannot be sure if the reader is having difficulty with the language in the passage or with the questions posed.

Pupils may score differently on tests of reading comprehension depending on whether the tests assess the amount of knowledge gained, the ability to answer questions that one couldn't answer before, or the strategies used in answering questions, as well as on whether immediate or deferred recall is required and on whether a test is an open- or closed-book task.

In order to learn more about how readers are processing and comprehending tests, it's a good idea to ask them to recall what they have read and then interpret the recall protocols in the light of both text and what is recalled. Patterns of distortion and omissions may indicate influence of the reader's background knowledge. Instead of relying on formal tests of comprehension, you will learn more about the comprehension of your learners by examining what they do, what they experience when reading, and how this experience is affected by the particular reading assignment. Find out what kinds of meaning reading has for different readers and observe what they do with a diversity of materials in many different situations—when reading, prior to reading, and subsequent to reading.

The following is an outline of questions to use in assessing whether pupils have the prerequisites for successful reading comprehension:

- Do pupils understand that they must attempt to make sense of text instead of focusing on reading as a decoding process? (Good readers know that reading should be meaningful.)
- Do pupils modify their reading strategies for different purposes? (For example, good readers know when to read for general impressions—*skim*—and when to read for specific information—*scan*.)

---

[5] B. F. Davis, "Research in the Comprehension of Reading," *Reading Research Quarterly* 3 (1968): 499–545.
[6] G. Hewitt, "A Critique of Research Methods in the Study of Reading Comprehension," *British Educational Research Journal* 8, no. 1 (1982): 9–21.

- Can pupils identify information in the text that is important to a particular theme, problem, or personal goal? (The ability to group propositions that belong to the gist of the text or to a given purpose requires a schema.)
- Can pupils tell when the descriptions of characters match the behavior of characters? (If they can do this, then they have knowledge of logical structure.)
- Do pupils notice statements that are incongruous with daily living and their own prior experience? (Recognizing alternative frameworks and experiencing conceptual conflict are prerequisites to change and accomodation to new ideas.)
- Do pupils know when they understand the text and when they do not? (Good readers ask themselves "Do I understand this?" "Could I repeat this?" "Where is all this leading?")
- Do pupils know what to do when they know they do not understand? (Rereading, continued reading for clarification, asking for help, and self-questioning are among the relevant strategies to be assessed.)

SCHEMA THEORY

Schema theory for teachers? Is it really necessary? How does it apply to my teaching? These might be questions you are asking as you read this.

Margaret Mead once said that education needs a new theory every few years. The theory does not have to be really novel or absolutely correct, but it must have at least some elements of novelty and correctness. A new perspective on reading is needed every once in a while to challenge you as a teacher to reconsider what you are doing—to rethink your purposes and methods, to review the latest research (even if the findings seem only to confirm the obvious), to examine new teaching practices, and perhaps to let you go away refreshed with the thought that you will be better able to solve some instructional problem that previously seemed insolvable.

Schema theory has special relevance for teachers of reading comprehension in that it questions the conventional view that pupils should learn to reproduce the statements found in text. That is, it casts doubt on the idea that books have explicit meanings that can be understood without the need for interpretive frameworks. According to schema theory, text is gobbledygook unless the reader can breathe meaning into it.

Ideally, pupils will read for their own purposes, relating the printed text to their own schemata and possibly modifying the text and their original schemata in the process. It follows that the pupil who does not apply schemata appropriately is going to have trouble learning and remembering the information found in textbooks.

Schemata serve several functions:

1. They are the slots for assimilating additional information—using a schema for *dessert,* it is easy to augment the familiar ice cream and cake with the new instance *flan.*
2. They help the reader see what is important. A schema for reading word problems tells us that we must attend to decisions about which operations to use in finding the answer.
3. They permit inferential elaboration. With a sports schema, we can mentally differentiate the size of the balls in such sentences as *The golfer hit the ball* and *The batter hit the ball.*
4. They aid in summarizing by helping the reader separate important from less important ideas. Schemata represent knowledge at all levels of abstraction—from major truths to the meaning of particular words. High-level schemata tend to be the more important ones. Readers with a schema for *fable* would in their summary of a fable give the moral more weight than any particular character, action, or event.
5. They aid in memory. It is our *interpretation* of what we read that is stored in memory. Hence, it is the interpretation rather than the text itself that we will recall. Our schema influences the interpretation in the first place and when activated helps us recall what we read.

As mentioned, schemata represent knowledge at all levels of generalization—from perspectives on the nature of the world, to views of what is meant by reading, to knowledge of patterns of written expression, to the meaning of a given term. Schemata are imbedded within schemata. For example, a schema for attending school would include top-level global generalizations about studying to learn and about socialization. Beneath this level would be more specific schemata—assignments, grades, teachers, principals, and peers. At the bottom level, there would be schemata for unique events—a first-grade teacher, a favorite book, a dear classmate. The powerful thing about schemata is that once any element in a network of schemata is specific, it can be understood as it relates to the entire complex. If *test* is mentioned within the schema for school, it will immediately be understood as a measure of someone's knowledge or aptitude and not confused with a trial, a shell of a mollusk, a reaction to a chemical, or a touchstone.

APPLYING SCHEMA THEORY IN BUILDING AND ACTIVATING PUPILS' BACKGROUND KNOWLEDGE

In order to comprehend written material, the reader must have schemata for defining the purpose of reading, identifying the organizational patterns of the material, and interpreting the key concepts. All of this is part of background knowledge. One of the most effective teaching devices for establishing such prerequisites and for activating appropriate background is the semantic map, an arrangement of vocabulary (or concepts) about a topic. These concepts are categorized in some way. The making of a semantic map is a procedure for building a bridge between the known and the new. The map provides the teacher with information on what the pupils know about a topic and gives the pupils anchor points to which the new concepts they will encounter can be attached.

Constructing a Semantic Map

Guidelines for helping pupils to make collectively a semantic map are as follows: Begin by asking pupils what they think of when they hear the word X (X is the topic they are going to read about). Free association is desirable. As pupils offer their associations, list the responses on the chalkboard. Try to put the associations into categories. For example, responses to *money* might be categorized into uses of money, kinds of money, denominations, consequences of having money, ways of earning it, and other associations.

Help the pupils label the categories and then ask them to read the selection to learn more about X. It is fine to encourage pupils to pose their own questions about what they want to learn about X from the text.

Next, after reading the selection, the class gives attention again to the set of categories and prereading questions related to X. Pupils at this time add new ideas acquired from their reading, correcting and augmenting the original map.

The resulting map is evidence of the pupils' preexisting schema, new learning from the text, and a relating of new and old knowledge. Discussion, posing of questions, and the relating of pupils' responses contribute to the success of semantic mapping.

Exhibit 1.1 depicts an initial, incomplete semantic map for the concept *gas*. Note in the exhibit how the more abstract superordinate concepts of matter to which the concept *gas* is related are placed at the top of the map. Schemata of a more concrete or subordinate level are placed lower.

A semantic map can be used to link pupils' basic concepts of the topic to both abstract schema and concrete examples. To illustrate, in the basic concept *dog, Fido* is at the concrete or subordinate level and *animal* is at an abstract of superordinate level. More pupils will be familiar with the term that represents a basic schema; so in building bridges from the known to the new, we usually start with topics at this level, then consider specific examples, and finally relate the term to the superordinate schema. If pupils need help with the concept of hierarchies, let them classify ideas

---

Exhibit 1.1   Initial Semantic Map for *Gas*

Gas
Related to
Molecular movement
Chemical changes
States of matter
Evaporation and condensation

Uses	*Kinds*	*Properties*
Healing	Natural	Expands
Illuminating	Acetylene	Fills space
Purifying	Helium	No volume
Putting people to sleep	Chlorine	No shape

---

about their favorite topics—sports, food, friends. While it's not essential for them to learn the words superordinate, coordinate, and subordinate, it can be useful. Let pupils decide why words like *color, texture,* and *shape* are superordinate to *blue, soft,* and *round.* More important, however, elicit the pupils' associations for the topic.

Additional explanation and illustrations of semantic mapping appear in Chapter 6 of this book. I would like to stress the importance of using the semantic mapping techniques in classrooms that include pupils from a variety of cultural backgrounds. You will find that minority-group pupils hold schemata for most topics, even though these schemata are not always conventional. The opportunity to relate their schemata to the topic of the text enables them to see relevance in what might otherwise be viewed as strange and aversive materials.

Activity 1.1   Constructing a Semantic Map

In order to assess the schematic background of your pupils and its appropriateness for the reading you expect them to do, have your class develop a semantic map for a topic in an upcoming lesson (such a topic might be *climate, happiness, computers,* or *reading*). Ask pupils to say what they think of when they hear the chosen word, then arrange responses to form a map. Pupils should label the categories of responses. Note whether or not pupils have schema at superordinate and subordinate levels.

You may wish to use the map as a means to generate pupils' questions. You may also wish to have pupils discuss and revise their map after reading the selection.

APPLYING SCHEMA THEORY IN ASSESSING PUPILS' COMPREHENSION OF STORIES

Analysis of children's story recall reveals which events in a selection are more memorable to them because of their interpretations. Analysis also indicates how well developed a child's sense of story structure is. Story structure is the explicit grammar, or pattern, by which stories are constructed. One such grammar, depicting episodic story structure, is that of Stein and Glenn.[7] It has these elements:

1. *Setting:* Introduction of the protagonist and information about the context in which story events will occur.
2. *Episode:*
a. *Initiating event* (cause for action and setting of goal).
b. *Internal response* (emotional reaction that causes the protagonist to initiate action).
c. *Attempts* (overt actions carried out in order to attain a goal).
d. *Consequence* (event, action, or end of tale, marking the attainment or nonattainment of the goal).
e. *Reaction* (expression of the protagonist's feelings about the outcome of the action or its broad consequences).

Children's schemata for story structure greatly influence their memory of what they read. Generally, older children are more competent in using their sense of story structure as an aid to factual recall. However, a schema for story structure can be developed. One way to develop the schema is to teach pupils to use story grammar in generating their own narratives. The writing of a story is an excellent way to enhance the ability to comprehend stories. Activity 1.2 (p. 13) will illustrate the technique.

Stephanie McConaughy has found that different types of story schemata are used by adults and children.[8] The schemata vary in both the components of information and the way the information is organized. She asked adults and children to read several stories and then to write summaries of them, telling only what they considered to be the most important parts for the meaning of the whole story. The summaries by young children showed a *simple descriptive schema*—beginning and ending components (the setting, initiating events, and resolution) and some details about intervening events and actions. Their schema answered the basic

---

[7] N. L. Stein and C. G. Glenn, "An Analysis of Story Comprehension in Elementary School Children," in *New Directions in Discourse Processing,* ed. R. O. Freedle (Hillsdale, N.J.: Erlbaum, 1979).
[8] S. H. McConaughy, "Using Story Structure in the Classroom," *Language Arts* 57 (February 1980): 157–65.

Activity 1.2   Using Story Grammar to Develop a Schema for Reading Narrative

---

First ask pupils to supply answers to the questions listed. Record their answers and then have them rewrite the answers as an original story.

1. *Setting:*
   a. Where will our story take place—at the beach, in an airplane, in a classroom? What is the place like?
   b. Who is the heroine or hero? What is she or he like? Describe.
2. *Episode:*
   a. What will happen?
   b. How will the heroine or hero (protagonist) feel about what happens?
   c. What does the protagonist want now? What does the protagonist plan to do? What does the protagonist do?
3. *Consequences:*
   a. What happens when the protagonist carries out the plan?
   b. Does the protagonist succeed or not?
4. *Reaction:*
   a. What did the protagonist learn from all this?
   b. What do we learn from this?

---

questions: What did X do in the story? What happened in the story? These children comprehended the stories at a literal level. Older children revealed an *information-processing schema;* they made inferences to supply missing information that logically fit in the story and supplied explanations to account for actions and events. The adult summaries represented a high-level, *social-inference* schema. The social-inference schema not only includes the basic components for actions and events, but also adds components that explain the motivation behind the characters' actions. This type of schema answers the question: Why did X do what he did in the story? Thus, the social-inference schema includes the goal of the character and the internal responses, thoughts, and subgoals that lead the character to action. Social-inference theory incorporates both psychological and physical causality to explain the sequence of actions and events. The addition of a moral to the story carries comprehension beyond the plane of the simple story schema to an inference about the author's intentions.

The evidence that children even up to the fifth grade spontaneously focus on more literal aspects suggests that pupils may need the help of specific problem questioning in order to focus on higher levels of comprehension. In kindergarten and first grade, questions about motivation may be inappropriate for testing comprehension. Children at these early levels are better at answering questions about simple details than they are at answering higher-level questions requiring inferences and justifications of outcomes. However, the teacher might draw out inferences about motivation *after* the literal aspects have been discussed.

Older children (sixth grade) could be asked to derive the theme themselves. They also could be asked questions that change the focus from actions and events to the goals and internal responses of the characters. Questions about the thoughts, feelings, and intentions of the characters, which focus on the motivation behind actions, might be appropriate for those with a social-inference schema.

Asking pupils to summarize a story has several advantages. The summary serves as a method for organizing the most important information. It gives the teacher a good firsthand picture of the nature of pupils' schema for a story, focusing on what the pupils think is important, rather than on what the teacher thinks is important. The teacher can then proceed, on the basis of the pupils' schema, to fill in missing components through questioning. The summary provides the schema for organizing basic information in memory from which elaborating details can be reconstructed. The schema, or framework, keeps children from becoming distracted by minor points as they retell a story. Encouraging children to develop and use their schemata should help them learn what to expect in a story and how to decide what it is important to remember.

Activity 1.3   Using the Summary of a Story to Reveal the Pupil's Schema for Stories

---

Ask pupils in your class to read and summarize a story. Analyze the summaries according to type of story schema:

Simple descriptive schema—the summary has beginning and ending components, including a setting, an initiating event, and a resolution.
Information-processing schema—the summary includes inferences to supply missing information that logically fits the story; and explanations to account for the causes of actions and events may be given.
Social-inference schema—in addition to the sequence of actions and events, this summary explains the motivation behind the characters' actions.

After completing your analysis, decide what the findings mean to you as a teacher. How might you take the results into consideration when assigning written material to children? How does the particular schema used influence what the pupils are learning from their reading? What follow-up questions might you ask in order to help children fill in missing story components?

Exhibit 1.2 is an illustration of the results obtained when this activity was undertaken at one primary school. Notice how attempts and major goals are better recalled than minor statements about setting.

Exhibit 1.2   Story Summaries

The Lion and the Mouse

A Lion was awakened from sleep by a Mouse running across his face. With a terrible roar, the Lion seized the Mouse with his paw and was about to kill him.

"Oh please," the Mouse begged. "Spare my life! I will be sure to repay your kindness."

The King of Beasts was so amused at the thought of a Mouse being able to help *him* that he let the frightened creature go.

Shortly afterward the Lion fell into a trap set by some hunters and was hopelessly caught in a net of strong ropes. In his misery the Lion roared so loudly that all the beasts in the forest heard him.

The Mouse recognized the roar of his former captor and ran to the place where the Lion lay trapped. At once the Mouse began to gnaw the ropes with his teeth. He gnawed rope after rope until at last the Lion was free.

"Thank you," said the grateful Lion. "I know now that *in time of need the weak may help the strong.*"

Source: Aesop's Fables, retold by Ann McGovern, Scholastic Book Services, New York, 1963, p. 42

The children listened while the teacher read *The Lion and the Mouse,* one of Aesop's fables (reproduced here). Then they wrote the story in their own words. Here are seven accounts, one from each Grade level of Primary School. Note the different meanings that the children have given the story. Is it possible to perceive any relationship between individual accounts and the types of story schema, i.e. simple descriptive schema, information-processing schema and social inference schema?

The Lion and the Mouse

A lion got trapped in a net and mighty mouse came and saved him

Prep.

The lion and the mouse

One day a lion was nesting under a tree. Under his paw
was a nut. a mouse saw the nut and tried to
get it but the lion awoke and was just
about to eat it but the mouse said don't
eat me. If your kind I will do something for
you but you must let me -go. So the lion
let the animal go and the mouse scamped off.
After a while the lion got trapped in a trap.
The mouse came to rescue the lion the
lion said thank you.

Grade 1

The Lion and the Mouse

There once was a Lion awoken by
a Mouse. The Lion was just about
to reach out his paw when the mouse
said Don't Do That I will Do anything
to rePay you back and one Day
he did. The lion got cought in a
trap and he to mouse heard him and the
and ran to him and nibbled roar
one rope after another and the Lion
was free.

Grade 2

The Lion and the Mouse

Once there was a Lion and a mouse. The mouse went walking with his eyes closed and walked right over the Lion. The Lion grabbed him. The mouse said I will help you any time you want me to. The Lion let him go. the next day. the Lion went for a walk. He fell into a net he roared. The mouse woke up and went running to the Lion. The mouse nibbled at the net it woke and the Lion got free.

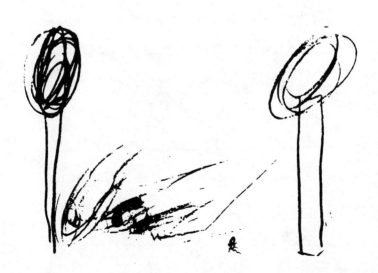

Grade 3

The Lion and the Mouse
Once upon a time there lived
a lion.
He went for a walk.
A mouse was running along
and banged into the lion
H roared.
The mouse said "Don't eat me.
If you don't eat I will help
you."
All right said the lion
The lion went for a walk.
He landed in a net.
The lion roared.
The mouse came running
and with his teeth he chewed
the net and he let the lion out.
The lion thanked the mouse
and they lived happily ever
after.

Grade 4

The Lion and the mouse

There was a little mouse and a big lion.
First the lion was awaked by the mouse and
the lion grabbed the mouse and the little
mouse said "Please let me go I will pay you
back with a favour." The Lion laughed,
ha ha ha you can't help me. So the lion
let him go. Late on the lion got stuck in a
net. The lion roared so loudly the whole
Jungle could hear him. The mouse recognized
his roar. The little mouse ran to the lion
and saw in the net a started growing on
the net. When he got the lion out of the
net the lion thanked him and said sometimes
little can help big.

Grade 5

THE LION & MOUSE

Once there was a lion.
He was sleeping. A mouse ran
across his nose. At once the lion
awoke and grabbed the helpless
mouse. The mouse said, " Let
me go. If you get into trouble
I may help you. So the mouse got
let go.
One day the lion got caught in a
net with very strong ropes, because
he was sad he roared as loudly
as he could. The mouse remembered
that roar and ran to save him. He
gnawed at every rope until the lion
was free and the mouse said,"If you
get a favor always return one."

Grade 6

APPLYING SCHEMA THEORY IN ASSESSING PUPILS' CONCEPTS OF READING

Pupils' concepts of reading may make a difference to whether or not they comprehend the text. It is thought that a major difference between good and poor comprehenders is the extent to which they are aware of the need to make sense of the text. Better comprehenders have come to know that stories should make sense and that reading instruction is a means to enhance their comprehension.

Beginning readers often do not know that reading is a communication process. Their schemata for reading may include slots for reading materials, for being read to, and for notions of how one reads—fast, fluently, and with expression. However, many children do not seem to know that an effort to make sense of the text is essential in reading.

Several investigators have ascertained children's schemata of reading at various grade levels. Denny and Weintraub asked first-graders, "What is reading?"[9] These researchers found that most did not know or gave an object-related response—for example, "It's reading a book." Only a few referred to reading as a process of learning new information. In answer to the question "What must you do to learn to read?" most children described a passive type of obedience or dependence on someone else. Only a few indicated that they had to take some action in learning to read, such as "read to myself" and "look at the pages."

Johns conducted studies to describe the relationship between pupils' concepts of reading and their reading achievement.[10] He asked three questions: "What is reading?" "What do you do when you read?" and "If someone didn't know how to read, what would you tell him to learn?" Johns found a positive correlation between the maturity of concepts of fourth- and fifth-grade children and their reading achievement.

The results of other studies also indicate that, across the grades, many students have little or no understanding of reading, most children identified word attack skills as the central concern in reading, and only a few referred to getting meaning from reading.

---

[9] T. Denny and S. Weintraub, "First Graders' Responses to Three Questions About Reading," *Elementary School Journal* 66 (1966): 441–48.
[10] J. Johns and D. Ellis, "Reading: Children Tell It Like It Is," *Reading World* 16, no. 2 (1976): 115–28.

Activity 1.4   Ascertaining Pupils' Schemata for Reading

Try to ascertain some of your pupils' knowledge of the purposes and nature of reading (their schemata for reading).

Use the following interview questionnaire. You will note that the first two questions are presented to relax the pupils and to affirm that you are interested in their ideas, not in "correct" responses. Question 3 attempts to tap the pupils' perceptions of themselves as readers and the understanding they have about how they might improve. Question 4 asks about the applicability of reading skills to materials other than books (signs, cereal boxes, T-shirts). Question 5 seeks to learn the students' awareness of how people learn to read. The last two questions are critical for determining whether or not the children see reading as a meaningful activity.

1. Are there some things you like about reading?
    Yes   No   What are they?
2. Are there some things you don't like about reading?
    Yes   No   What are they?
3. Are you a good reader?
    Yes   No   Why do you think so?
4. Can you read if you don't have a book?
    Yes   No   Why?   Why not?
5. What things does a person have to learn how to do in order to be a good reader?
6. What is reading?
7. Why do people read?

Question 6 provides information on the pupils' schema for reading. Responses such as "reading means reading a book" should be grouped under the heading *object focus*. Responses referring to the mechanics of reading may be grouped under *decoding focus*. Responses that fall under a *meaning focus* are of two types: (1) activities that stress "bottom-up" strategies for getting information (learning word meanings, putting words together, understanding sentences and stories, remembering what is read); and (2) activities that imply a critical or reflective approach to text (interpreting signs and symbols, thinking about what is read, enjoying other peoples' lives, learning about people and the world).

Once you have the responses categorized under object, decoding, or meaning focus, think about their implications. Is there more need for frequent reading outside school, for expanding vocabularies, for increasing the knowledge base, or for personal involvement with text?

Exhibit 1.3 reproduces responses to the questionnaire above from children six to twelve years of age who attend a two-teacher rural school. From the children's comments you may perceive that the school's reading program features a commercially prepared, structured, sequenced treatment of reading skills with basal readers and pupils' record books. This explains the children's references to the program, tests, and practice books.

Exhibit 1.3   Responses to Reading Concepts Questionnaire

---

1. Are there some things you like about reading?

I like reading because it is fun trying
to solve the mystery in some novels.

when I read books
to myself.

The practice book and the tests.

2. Are there some things you don't like about reading?

No because it's fun.

decause it annoys me   Sometimes it's
boring

when we do hard pages
in our practice book

3. Are you a good reader?

(No) Because I sound like a robot and
I stop in the middle of a sentence

Yes I think I am a good reader
because I read every night

4.   Can you read if you don't have a book?

You find words
in books and   because   there are
if you don't love   Signs to read
books then no
words to read   I can't see the words

5.   What things does a person have to learn to do in order to be a good reader?

If you want to be a good reader
you would learn how too work out
words that you don't no

To stop   at a full stop and to
put expression into it.

6.   What is reading?

Something that ^is thought   A program
of and is writen on
paper and is said   the time when you
again in by being read   read your books

7.   Why do people read?

people read to fill in time and find
out things .

to learn about
something or for   to hear Stores
the joy.

SUMMARY

The topics of Chapter 1 applied primarily to introductory phases in teaching reading—the beginning of a course of instruction and the introducing of particular reading selections and lessons. Accordingly, the chapter emphasized the importance of finding out about the pupils' prior experience and their expectations from reading as well as assessing their schema for story or exposition and determining their background knowledge of the topic to be read. A central point is that the reader must take part in deriving and creating meaning from written material. Hence, the chapter suggested that the teacher should not only provide background knowledge for a selection but also help the reader activate existing schemata, using them as a bridge from the familiar to the unfamiliar.

Strategies for both assessing and activating schema—semantic mapping, story writing, story retelling, interviewing—were featured, and activities and materials were suggested for trying out these strategies in your own situation.

Useful Reading

Adams, M. J., and A. Collins. "A Schema-Theoretic View of Reading." Technical Report no. 32. Urbana: Center for the Study of Reading, University of Illinois, April 1977.

Anderson, R. C. "The Notion of Schemata and the Educational Enterprise." In *Schooling and the Acquisition of Knowledge,* ed. R. C. Anderson, R. J. Spiro, and W. E. Montague. Hillsdale, N.J.: Erlbaum, 1977.

Baker, L., and A. L. Brown. "Cognitive Monitoring in Reading." In *Understanding Reading Comprehension,* ed. J. Flood. Newark, Del.: IRA (in press).

Canney G., and P. Winograd. "Schemata for Reading and Reading Comprehension Performance." Technical Report no. 120. Urbana: Center for the Study of Reading, University of Illinois, April 1979.

Greeno, J. G. "Psychology of Learning 1960–80." *American Psychologist* 35, no. 8 (1980): 713–28.

Guthrie, J. T. "Research Views: Story Comprehension." *Reading Teacher* 30 (1977): 574–77.

McConaughy, S. H. "Using Story Structure in the Classroom." *Language Arts* 57 (February 1980): 157–65.

Mandler, J. M., and N. S. Johnson. "Remembrance of Things Parsed: Story Structure and Recall." *Cognitive Psychology* 9 (1977): 111–51.

Nelson, K. "Cognitive Development and the Acquisition of Concepts." In *Schooling and the Acquisition of Knowledge,* ed. R. C. Anderson, R. J. Spiro, and W. E. Montague. Hillsdale, N.J.: Erlbaum, 1977.

Rumelhart, D. E. "Notes on a Schema for Stories." In *Representation and Understanding,* ed. D. G. Bobrow and A. Collins. New York: Academic Press, 1975.

2 Active Readers

Overview

Where does meaning lie? Schema theory posits that knowledge is packaged into units. These units are schemata. Comprehension is possible when features of a text—words, sentences, paragraphs—are matched with slots or place holders in the reader's schemata. Often, the slots are filled by inferences rather than by the information directly stated. The reader's mental schemata, or knowledge frameworks, interact with the textual clues to create meaning. The reader does more than encode print, as though the message could stand by itself. On the other hand, the reader's schemata change as the text provides new information that is assimiliated with existing knowledge structures.

In Chapter 1 you found that persons learning to read have developed schemata about reading. Some of these schemata are more useful than others. Pupils may fail to become independent readers because they have schematized reading as a passive activity or an activity in which they must catalog bits of information verbatim in order to answer a teacher's questions.

In this chapter you are invited to examine teaching practices that aim at helping children become active readers—readers who see reading as meaningful communication. Meaning does not lie in text but in the interaction between what the author has written and the reader's own background and expectations. Of course, the reader's interpretation is subject to evaluation. Readers may be asked to show how the meaning they derived corresponds to text, what assumptions underlie their meaning, and what consequences follow from such a meaning.

FROM ANSWERING TO ASKING QUESTIONS

Harry Singer has long been interested in a process for teaching comprehension that departs from the traditional practice of asking pupils questions before, during, and after reading.[1] His process of active comprehension teaches pupils to formulate their own questions. The purpose for teaching such a process is to help pupils acquire a schema of reading in which they have purpose and then encourage a dynamic interaction between reader and author.

In teaching active comprehension, the teacher asks a question to get a question, not an answer. For example, a kindergarten teacher may hold up a picture for the children to look at. Instead of asking questions about the picture that yield answers such as "Who is on the bike?" or "What is going to happen?" the teacher says, "Look at the picture. What would you like to know about the picture?" The questions children ask in response to the question are often surprising.

Pupil-initiated questions (made in response to the study of pictures, headings, and other aspects of the text) reflect the pupils' perceptions, backgrounds, and cognitive development. Some children may first ask about details and then go on to the main idea. Others may start with the theme before progressing to details. In the above example from the kindergarten, children might say such things as: "Why is the boy on the bicycle?" "Does the little girl see the boy on the bike?" "Will they crash?"

Questions may be referred to the class, and then the teacher might ask: "What would you like to know about what happened next?" "How would you avoid the crash?" The latter question directs thinking toward a solution to a problem. After several solutions have been elicited, the teacher might say, "Let's turn the page, read, and see how the person who drew these pictures (the author) solved the problem." After understanding the author's solution, the teacher initiates an evaluation of it: "Is this the best way to stop a crash?" Thus, even in the kindergarten, children develop critical and affective schemata.

[1] Harry Singer, "Active Comprehension," *Reading Teacher* 31, no. 8 (1978): 901–908.

Questions can be elicited from pupils in many ways. One third-grade teacher introduced a book by having someone read the title and then asking pupils what they wanted to find out about the book. Another teacher arranged a competitive situation in which the class was divided into two groups, with two pupils at the chalkboard to write down questions. The pupils filled the chalkboard and then tried to outdo each other in answering their own questions, stimulated by the title and first paragraph.

Exhibit 2.1 is a lesson used by Singer in teaching active comprehension.

Exhibit 2.1   Lesson in Teaching Active Comprehension

Passage

"Filming a Cannibal Chief" by Osa Johnson

My husband and I wanted to make a moving picture of savages, and Martin finally decided on Malekula, second largest of the New Hebrides Islands. We started from Sydney, Australia on a small ship. Soon a storm of warning broke around us.

Teacher-student interaction

Teacher questions to elicit student questions:
Look at the title. What questions could you ask just from the title alone?

Student questions on the title:
How do you film a cannibal chief? (Often implicit in this question is the idea of how do you film a cannibal chief and get away with it.)
Were they successful?
Why film a cannibal chief?

Teacher techniques for eliciting questions in the paragraph:
What would you like to know about Martin?

Student questions:
Who is Martin?
Is Martin the husband?
Why did Martin decide?
Did Martin have trouble making up his mind?
Is Martin deliberative?
Are there many places where cannibals still live?

Exhibit 2.1   *(Continued)*

Teacher question:
   Is there anything you would like to know about the relationship between the
   writer and Martin?

Student questions:
   Is she frustrated by Martin's indecision?
   Is he the domineering person in their relationship?
   Is she a nagging type of person?

Teacher question:
   Does the ship make you wonder about the trip?

Student questions:
   Why were they going in a small ship?
   How small was the small ship?
   Why didn't the author describe the ship?

Teacher question:
   Look at the last sentence. What questions pop into your mind as you read
   that sentence?

Student questions:
   What is a storm of warning?
   What kind of danger are they about to encounter?
   Will they survive?

Source: Harry Singer, "Active Comprehension," *Reading Teacher* 31, no. 8 (1978): 906.

Russell Stauffer also has advocated teaching pupils to raise questions in order that they may become reading-thinking scholars.[2] He has proposed a teaching strategy called *group-directed reading-thinking activity* (DRTA). A teacher's plan of action in the DRTA is (1) to activate pupils' thoughts before reading by asking such questions as "What do you think?" (2) to agitate reflective thought by asking, "Why do you think so?" and (3) to require evidence in support of the conclusion in the form of references to the text and peer judgments regarding the force of the arguments.

---

[2] Russell G. Stauffer, "Strategies for Reading Instruction," in *45th Yearbook,* ed. Malcolm Douglas (Claremont, Calif.: Claremont Reading Conference, 1981), pp. 58–74.

DRTA lessons allow pupils to work in small groups that read the same material but from different perspectives and for different purposes. Some purposes may be of group origin, and others may be individual. Pupils compare and contrast their predictions and paths to answers before reading. Answers derived from the reading and thinking are subject to evaluation.

HELPING PUPILS ASK QUESTIONS

One strategy for attaining the goal of active questioning has been termed the *phase-in–phase-out* strategy. Here, the teacher phases in the questioning process by taking the first step in modeling questions that are appropriate to the content. The teacher also offers additional information about the content to be read or explains more about the topic.

Some knowledge of the content to be read is necessary in order to generate appropriate questions. Once pupils have an idea of the kinds of questions that can be asked about different types of content (expository writing, narrative prose), they are formed into groups to ask each other questions regarding the material to be read. Final phasing out occurs when the pupils ask and answer appropriate questions on their own.

Anne Maria Palincsar and Ann Brown have had success in teaching questioning routines to children who were adequate decoders but poor comprehenders.[3] Their procedures were based on A. V. Manzo's *request method,* by which the pupils and the teacher take turns in asking each other questions regarding a passage.[4] Palincsar concentrated on two types of comprehension questions to use while reading: *interpretations* (What is happening now? What is causing it?) and *predictions* (What will happen next?)

Working with individuals, she took turns with each child in leading dialogues over segments of text. Both the teacher and the child read a paragraph, and then one assumed the role of dialogue leader, asking questions about the main idea and about how the information might be grouped together. The dialogue leader also asked questions about what was presently happening in the selection and what might occur in remaining passages. Then the roles were reversed.

At first pupils had difficulty assuming the role of dialogue leader when their turns came. The teacher had to construct paraphrases and questions for the pupils to mimic. Only after several sessions did pupils themselves provide paraphrases and questions of sophistication.

[3] A. M. Palincsar, "A Corrective Feedback and Strategy Training Program to Improve the Comprehension of Poor Readers" (Unpublished manuscript, University of Illinois, 1981).
[4] A. V. Manzo, "Improving Reading Comprehension Through Reciprocal Questioning" (Doctoral dissertation, Syracuse University, 1968).

Children who received training in the questioning routines greatly improved in their ability to answer comprehension questions. This training was even more effective when it followed a procedure by which pupils first read silently and then answered questions. Subsequently, the teacher praised correct responses and guided the pupils back into the paragraphs in which the answers could be found.

The technique of teaching questioning by a reciprocal game need not follow the teacher-and-one-child approach taken in the above studies, which may not be practical for classroom use. Instead, a few teacher-trained pupils can be paired with naive peers for playing the questioning game.

CONSEQUENCES OF QUESTIONING BY PUPILS

In classroom situations there is sometimes a problem with self-generated questions. Pupils may focus on one detail or aspect of a comprehension test or quiz on the material. Although it is important that pupils answer their own questions, a teacher may want evidence that they comprehended what others have found valuable and what the teacher expects readers to learn from given material. Hence, pupils are taught to generate questions that will be most useful in deriving commonly expected meanings from given subject matter. Chapter 8 contains illustrations of the kinds of questions that will help pupils organize and integrate text content as well as the kinds of questions that illuminate ideas of central importance to the author.

There is research supporting the idea that pupils who are taught to actively comprehend resist the narrowing effect of some teacher-posed questions. Active readers have been found to perform better on literal, interpretive, and general comprehension tests than pupils who have been restricted to teachers' prereading and postreading questions.[5] Fifth-graders using the reciprocal questioning procedure (the pupils asked the teacher a question for each teacher-posed question they answered) performed better on an interpretation test than pupils in a group in which only the teacher posed questions.[6]

Pupils learn to imitate teachers' questions. Questions asked at interpretive and applicative levels stimulate higher cognitive processes than do factual questions. It might be better, therefore, to help pupils initiate broad questions that have several acceptable answers instead of only narrow questions that have a single right answer. One cautionary note,

[5] A. Rhodes, "Active Comprehension," (Unpublished research, University of California, Riverside, 1977).
[6] J. P. Helfeldt and R. Lalik, "Reciprocal Student-Teacher Questioning," *Reading Teacher* 3 (1976): 283–87.

however, is that the use of broad divergent questions with children who do not have the schemata for answering these questions will result in little understanding.

EFFECTS OF QUESTIONING BY TEACHERS

The topic of prereading and postreading questions and their effect on comprehension is treated differently by cognitivists, who see the reader as creating a context for interpreting the author's message, and behaviorists, who favor reinforcement for correct responses and antecedent manipulations such as modeling and prompting.

The practice of questioning before reading (prequestioning) is a common one. Studies evaluating the practice from a behavioristic view show that pupils do better at answering test questions after reading if they have been asked the *same* questions earlier, the prereading questions serving as attention-getting devices or hints on what to look for.[7]

The cognitivist's view emphasizes the use of test questions that elicit more general responses, not verbatim recall nor direct matches to prequestions. Prequestions are regarded by the cognitivist as aids to processing what is read. Accordingly, the questions should force the pupil to process relevant aspects of the text in useful ways: "How will you use the information in your own project?" Questions that force a child to review or summarize the material improve comprehension. Many teachers have intuitively helped children acquire the schema of reading as a meaningful activity by asking such questions as: "Can you get into an argument about what you read? On whose side of the argument are you? Why?" "When you read this, what ideas are not actually put into words?" "What is the story *really* about?" "Who might like it and why?"

The use of prequestions as a device to activate the learner's schema is another way in which questions aid in the processing of information. Asking pupils to find details that support or refute a general idea makes for more effective processing than asking pupils to recall specific details. Just as comprehension of a selection is improved when the reader attends to a descriptive title, picture, or heading before reading a passage, so questions make the selection more comprehensible.

To better understand how questions can activate schema, first try to derive meaning from the drawing in Exhibit 2.2 without reading the question that accompanies it. Then read the question and see whether the drawing means something different.

---

[7] L. M. Reder, "The Role of Elaboration in the Comprehension and Retention of Prose: A Critical Review," *Review of Educational Research* 50 (Spring 1980): 5–53.

Exhibit 2.2   Activating Schemata

Can you see both an old woman and a young woman in this drawing?

RELATING CHILDREN'S BACKGROUNDS
TO THEIR READING

Children need to be aware that it is necessary to use what they already know in order to understand the text—that the knowledge they already have can help them in their reading.

The attitude that one knows nothing about what is to be read has been described by Pearson and Johnson as the "Charlie Brown syndrome."[8]

[8] David P. Pearson and Dale D. Johnson, *Teaching Reading Comprehension* (New York: Holt, Rinehart, and Winston, 1978), p. 192.

Recall what Charlie Brown does whenever he gets a new book. Before he even looks at the book, he counts the pages—625 pages—"I'll never learn all that!" He is defeated before he starts, before he has had a chance to realize that he does not have to learn *all* that. It is not *all* new. He already knows something about it. He has not given himself the chance to learn what he already knows about what he is supposed to know.

The Charlie Brown syndrome is common with readers from non-English-speaking cultures, who often regard activities in English as strange and incomprehensible.

A good way to overcome pupils' reluctance to apply what they know to the unfamiliar is for the teacher to elicit from the pupils their ideas about the topic, theme, concept, or other organizing element in the selection to be read. The semantic mapping activity in Chapter 1 serves well in this connection. When pupils tell what a topic means to them and relate their experiences with the topic, they establish an anticipatory set. It enables them to state the questions they want answered by the selection, to say what they expect to find, and to guess about the way the information will be presented.

However, it is not enough for pupils to relate their experience to a topic before reading. Their background must be brought to bear at all phases of the reading process. Kathryn Au has had unusual success in helping minority children achieve in reading by making the children's past experience an integral part of the entire lesson.[9] Au's cognitive training lessons are composed of three different kinds of sequences—an *experience* sequence for eliciting background, a *text* sequence for determining what sense children are making from the text, and a *relationship* sequence by which children contrast their own experiences with what they read.

Exhibit 2.3 describes and illustrates a lesson (taught to second-graders who are members of a minority group) that uses the experience-text-relationship (ETR) method.

In Au's ETR method, the children practice expressing complex thoughts; and during the process, the teacher gets an idea of which steps are easy or difficult for individual children. The teacher's interaction with pupils helps them to integrate features of the story with their existing store of knowledge. Over time the children learn to apply the method by themselves. Those who have interacted frequently with a teacher in ETR lessons show better comprehension when reading their own than children who have not had this opportunity.

Using children's own backgrounds does not prevent the teacher from providing other background knowledge. It has been found that if teachers

[9] Kathryn Au, "Using the Experience-Text-Relationship Method with Minority Children," *Reading Teacher* 32 (March 1979): 678–79.

Exhibit 2.3   Lesson Using the Experience-Text-Relationship Method

---

Experience

In an *E* or experience sequence, the teacher has the children discuss experiences they have had, or knowledge they have, which is related in some way to the story. In the following example of an *E* sequence, the teacher is having each of the children talk about what she would do if she had a frog.

Teacher: Okay, let's think if we could do anything else with a frog. What would you do, Shirley?

Ann: I wouldn't touch the legs. Yuck.

Shirley: I would put it in a bucket.

Teacher: You would put it in a bucket. Okay, that's something different.
What would you do with it?

Shirley: (Inaudible)

Ann: Yeah, you eat the legs?

Teacher: Okay, Shirley might even eat it. Good, you can eat frog, can't you?

Text

After this first part of the lesson, in which the children share their experiences, the teacher has them read short parts of the story, usually a page or two, asking them questions about the content after each section is read. These are the *T* or text sequences. Sometimes the children show misunderstandings which the teacher must work hard to correct, as in the following *T* sequence.

Teacher: Shirley, why did you say Freddy laughed? Okay, read the part that you said—when Freddy laughed.

Shirley: [Reading] "I would take it fishing. Freddy laughed."

Teacher: Okay, who says, "I would take it fishing"?

Nathan: Mr. Mays.

Teacher: Mr. Mays. And why did Freddy laugh?

Ann: Because maybe he didn't—maybe he didn't know that he was going to use the frog.

Teacher: No, he laughed for another reason. Ellie? Who can read that?

Ellie: Because—'cause Mr. Mays didn't know what to do with the frog. That's all he could think was—he didn't know that he could use frogs was—was a bait. That's why Freddy laughed.

Teacher: Okay, wait a minute. That's not the reason Freddy laughed.

Nathan: Frogs can't fish.

Teacher: Right. Okay. Mr. Mays says, "I don't have a frog, but if I did, I'd take it fishing," and Freddy thinks, hah, going fishing with the frog sitting down with the fishing pole?

Relationship

The final category is the *R* or relationship sequence. In *R* sequences the teacher attempts to draw relationships for the children between the content of the story discussed in the *T* sequences and their outside experience and knowledge. In this example of an *R* sequence, the teacher provides the opportunity for the children to contrast their own knowledge about what can be used as bait in fishing with an idea presented in the story.

Teacher: Did you know before this that fish like to eat frogs?

Group: Nooo.

Teacher: I didn't—I never heard of using frogs for bait. Do you think they really do?

Nathan: Yeah.

Exhibit 2.3   (*Continued*)

Teacher: You think so.
Ann: My daddy—my daddy—use bread.
Teacher: Yeah, some people use bread. What else do you use for bait?
Shirley: Fish.
Teacher: Sometimes you use smaller fishes.

The *E, T,* and *R* sequences show the teacher's efforts to guide the children systematically through the cognitive processes related to understanding a written story. The teacher in the examples is a skillful questioner, particularly adept at leading the children to the . . . answers, rather than telling them the answers.

Source: Au, 1979, p. 678

offer such knowledge, pupils will remember more of the material.[10] By way of example, some children in various grades were given information about a fictitious tribe called the "Targa," while others learned about people from Spain. Later, all the children read a story about a young boy from the Targa tribe, and no mention was made of what they had studied previously. Those who had received the relevant background information recalled more information from their reading.

DIFFERENCES BETWEEN PUPILS' AND AUTHORS' PURPOSES

Active readers seek printed material in order to meet a variety of needs— to solve problems, to further their interests, to escape psychologically, to help others, to protect economic stakes, to seek knowledge, to satisfy curiosity, to improve themselves, to find spiritual inspiration. In so doing, they bring many purposes to their reading. On the other hand, authors have their own purposes in communicating certain information. The problem of getting the purposes of the reader and the purposes of the author to interact is a real one.

F. D. Flower tells how he failed to find what he wanted in a particular work, even though he was convinced that the author had something to say relevant to his purposes.[11] Flower was interested in interpreting the symbols poets use in describing dreams. He thought that the psychoanalytical theories of Sigmund Freud might help, because he knew that Freud placed great emphasis on his patients' dreams. Flower sought a copy of Freud's *The Interpretation of Dreams*. He looked down the list of con-

---

[10] A. C. Brown et al., "Instruction of a Thematic Idea in Children's Comprehension and Retention of Stories," *Child Development* 49 (1977): 1458–66.
[11] F. D. Flower, *Reading to Learn* (London: British Broadcasting Corporation, 1970).

tents and referred to the index. Then he saw that in spite of the title the work was no handbook to the meaning of dreams, as might be found in some popular magazines from time to time, but a very full account with many examples of what dreams are and why they occur. Flower read through Chapter 3, "A Dream Is a Fulfillment of a Wish," and glanced at Chapter 6, "The Dream's Work," especially Section E, "Representation by Symbols in Dreams." Although he found these parts interesting, he did not discover anything to help him interpret the symbols used by poets. Obviously, Flower had to make up his mind whether to continue digging into the book to see if he could find what he was looking for or to give up and look elsewhere. Freud's book is fascinating, but Flower's time was limited; so he put *Interpretation of Dreams* to one side until another time.

Some authorities recommend that when readers' purposes for reading have been frustrated, they should not do as Flower did but should modify their goals and adjust their original purposes as they read. Perhaps the reading goals of children are not well formed; in continued reading, they may be able to find better purposes.

Readers can satisfy their own purpose even when the author has a different one. Mature readers have learned, for instance, how to "raid" texts for the information they want, selecting only the information that meets their special purposes. They know when raiding is appropriate and when it is not. They may use the technique of scanning, in which they anticipate what type of answer to their question is likely to be found in the text. When scanning, they don't look for or recall any information other than the answer to the predetermined question. Indexes, tables of contents, titles, and headings are used in searching for the right places to scan. "Leafing through a text" and sampling introductory and concluding paragraphs are all part of the technique.

What responsibility do teachers have for helping children pose questions that are answerable from the reading selection at hand? What should children be taught about how best to seek answers to their own questions through printed materials?

SCHEMATA FOR COMMUNICATING
WITH AUTHORS

Although the main variable determining whether a reader will comprehend a specific communication is background knowledge relevant to the content, schemata that match the author's organizational pattern also help the reader interpret the message by enabling him or her to anticipate the author's purpose. In Activity 2.2, to follow, and again in Chapter 8, you will have the opportunity to develop your own schemata for patterns commonly used by authors. Five such patterns are the sharing-experience pattern, the question-answer pattern, the imparting-information pattern, the opinion-reason pattern, and the substantiated-fact pattern. Each pattern signals a purpose, thus indicating how the material should be read—slowly, with careful attention to details; quickly, to gain general impressions; or merely to answer a specific question.

We can recognize the sharing-experience pattern by asking whether the author is telling about some first-hand experience. The use of personal pronouns—*I, we, our,* and *us*—indicates that the material represents this schema ("I shall never forget that most frightful hurricane"). Once children recognize this pattern, they should know that they may read it as rapidly as they wish, for there are no detailed facts to recall. With material written in the sharing-experience pattern, we may relax and read quickly, enjoying the author's experiences.

The question-answer pattern is easy to recognize and easy to read. We just have to read the question and then glance through the text until we find the answer. The use of the question helps the reader understand the author's purpose at once, making it unnecessary to formulate personal questions and motives for reading. Whenever titles, headings, or paragraphs are in question format, you know that the author's purpose is to answer the question. An example of the question-answer pattern is: "Why test? To ascertain where one is, to chart progress, and to identify areas that remain to be explored."

A third pattern is the imparting-information pattern. Unlike the previous two, it requires careful, detailed reading—at least, it does if the reader decides the material is important to read. As implied by the name, material written in this pattern contains many factual details. The following example, which summarizes the way heat recovery systems retrieve and reuse heat, illustrates the pattern. Notice the many different details packed into a single passage.

> The system creates a thermal path that transports heat escaping up an exhaust duct to a cold incoming air stream. The key component is the heat pipe. The pipe is a closed metal envelope containing a capillary wick and a small amount of liquid within a sealed cylinder. When the end of the pipe is heated, the energy changes the liquid to a gas and drives it to the opposite end. There the vapor condenses, releasing it for warming incoming cold air. The liquid then returns to the wick to repeat the cycle.

The opinion-reason pattern can be read with little time or effort, providing one can recognize it. Clues to this pattern are found in such phrases as, "in my opinion," "as I see it," "I believe," "I think," or "common sense suggests." Material written in this pattern should be read rapidly to first get an understanding of the author's opinion and to then find the reasons the author offers in support of the opinion. An example follows on page 42.

Activity 2.1   Pupil-Initiated Questions versus Teacher-Initiated Questions—a Classroom Study

This activity should help you to find out what is involved in eliciting prereading questions from pupils and to assess the value of the practice.

Select a fresh story or other reading material for your pupils. From this material prepare four questions, two of which are factual or literal (the reader should supply or recognize some item of information given in the passages) and two of which require the making of inferences (the reader should state a relationship between elements of the passages that is implied but not explicitly stated). These four questions will constitute the teacher-initiated questions for the selection.

Randomly choose half of your pupils to generate their own questions to be answered by reading the selection. Introductory paragraphs, titles, pictures, and other features of the selection may be used to help these pupils generate four questions, which will constitute the pupil-initiated questions. Summarize the pupil-generated questions and then let the pupils who proposed them read the selection. Next present the teacher-generated questions to those pupils who did *not* participate in posing questions and ask them to read the selection. After a day's delay and without allowing the children an opportunity to reread, administer a test consisting of both the teacher-generated and the pupil-generated questions. Both groups of pupils should get the same test.

Score this eight-item test and then analyze the results. What questions might these results answer? Here are some questions you could ask: Was there any difference between the recall scores of the pupils who were in the question-generating group and those who were given the teacher-generated questions? Did the pupils in the question-generating group answer more of their own questions correctly than pupils who were not in this group? Did the prereading focus on generating questions interfere with the question-initiating pupils' ability to answer teacher-generated questions—that is, did the narrower focus interfere with concomitant or incidental learning?

As an alternative to the general procedure of this study, you may have *each* child in one group generate his or her own questions. You might then compare responses to one child's questions with responses to the questions generated by the teacher or by other pupils. Other studies have found that, compared with answering questions asked by other children, asking one's own questions facilitated memory. Also, manipulation of instruction might be undertaken to see how the learners perceive their task. For example, you may wish to compare the effect of telling children to read *only* in order to answer the given questions with the effect of telling them to answer the questions but also to learn as many other things as possible from the selection. Pupils' questions might be compared with teachers' questions with respect to whether or not they can be answered by reading the selection and whether or not they show a balance between factual (literal) and inferential levels of comprehension.

Examination of the kinds of questions posed by pupils and teachers alike might reveal whether those of either origin would lead learners to process the information so that it would be learned and retained.

Activity 2.2   Recognizing an Author's Pattern and Adjusting Your Reading Approach to It

Now that you have considered five commonly used patterns, see if you can recognize the patterns in text and can read each selection at the speed demanded by its pattern.
Check the answer that corresponds to the author's pattern and then read the selection at the speed appropriate for the pattern.

1. sharing-experience ☐   question-answer ☐   imparting-information ☐
    opinion-reason ☐   substantiated-fact ☐
    My bet is that "The Stewarts" will prove a success on public television as did "The Sandland Saga" nearly ten years ago. For one thing, the series is better than the "Saga," just as Jay is a superior novelist to Scott. Consider, too, that "The Sandland" series was filmed in black and white, and "The Stewarts" is in faultless color.
    The script, written by Douglas Hunter, performs miracles in translating the intricate plot of five novels, set in the period 1735–65, into a seamless tapestry. The acting is nearly impeccable, at least in the four episodes I saw.

2. sharing-experience ☐   question-answer ☐   imparting-information ☐
    opinion-reason ☐   substantiated-fact ☐
    Intake air temperature varies widely from cold on starting to hot during regular operation. The density of the air varies with temperature change. Unfortunately, automotive carburetors are not able to meter fuel to match density changes and to maintain a near ideal air/fuel ratio. Since engines operate most of the time with warm or hot air, carburetors' jetting is set to give the proper ratio under these conditions. This leaves the cold range somewhat lean. To compensate, a method was devised to provide warm air more quickly. Under cold operating conditions intake air is drawn over an exhaust manifold to warm it prior to mixing with fuel.

3. sharing-experience ☐   question-answer ☐   imparting-information ☐
    opinion-reason ☐   substantiated-fact ☐
    The slow learner—what are his characteristics and needs? The slow learner tends to have poorer reasoning ability than the normal child. He is slow to see cause and effect relationships, to make inferences, and to generalize.
    Short attention span seems to typify this group of learners. However, the short attention span is often due to poor instruction rather than to a defect in the slow learner. When materials are interesting and when success is possible, the attention span of the slow learner increases. Unlike brighter persons, slow learners do not learn incidentally, as a rule. Careful planning by a teacher is a must to facilitate their learning. The slow learner needs immediate goals rather than deferred ones. He must see a reason here and now for engaging

Activity 2.2 **(Continued)**

in a task. He needs a stimulating environment where he has many
things to talk about.

4. sharing-experience ☐   question-answer ☐   imparting-information ☐
   opinion-reason ☐   substantiated-fact ☐
   I heard some singing coming from the bathroom, or perhaps I should
   say reverberating. In the past when this had happened, I had been very
   disturbed about it and outlawed the music because it is Lucy's most
   glaring symptom and the one which made me realize that there was
   something wrong with her. She would listen to her records sometimes
   all day, during which time she would be in a trancelike state, unable to
   speak, hear or eat. This time I paid attention to the words and was
   surprised to learn that the song tells the story of a girl who runs away
   from home, and the chorus tells of the parents' consequent
   bewilderment. I then knew that the songs I had forbidden probably
   contained important messages and clues to Lucy's problems.

5. sharing-experience ☐   question-answer ☐   imparting-information ☐
   opinion-reason ☐   substantiated-fact ☐
   Language is the source of logic. In fact, the logic of the logicians is
   itself nothing but generalized syntax and semantics. Evidence for this
   conclusion is found in studies comparing normal children with deaf
   mutes, who have not had the benefit of articulate language but are in
   possession of complete sensory-motor schemes, and with blind
   persons, whose situation is the opposite.
       The results indicate a systematic delay in the emergence of logic
   in the deaf mute and an even longer delay (up to four years) among
   blind children. Being born blind hampered the development of
   sensory-motor schemes and verbal co-ordinations are not sufficient to
   compensate for the delay.

   Answers

1. The first passage is in the opinion-reason pattern. You should have
   read it quickly.
2. The second passage is an instance of information-imparting. It should
   have been read slowly and with attention to details.
3. The third passage is an example of the question-answer pattern, a
   pattern that frames the question for you, making it easy to read quickly
   for the answer.
4. The fourth passage is in the sharing-experience pattern, to be read at
   your highest speed.
5. The fifth passage is an example of the substantiated-fact pattern. You
   should have read the selection slowly and decided whether or not the
   author gave sufficient evidence for the conclusion presented.

If you want children to feel at home in school, put them in an old building, not a spanking new one. I think only an older building gives the impression of having been lived in long enough to understand the troubles of life. It has gone through and survived a lot. That is why it is preferable to adapt an old building with a lived-in feeling for the purposes of a school.

The fifth pattern is the substantiated-fact pattern. You can identify it by looking for a conclusion or statement of fact followed by substantiation in the form of observation, experiment, or other data. Material written in this pattern should be read carefully and slowly. A suggested reading procedure is: (1) understand the author's conclusions; (2) challenge the author to prove it; and (3) read on to see if the proof is sufficient.

SUMMARY

The topics of Chapter 2 applied to the initiation of reading activity—the setting of goals, the asking of questions, and the making of predictions. The relation of this initiating activity to processing text, to monitoring, and to integrating text with personal experience was shown.

Efficient readers approach reading tasks in a more active, strategic, and flexible fashion than poor readers. Poor readers' passivity is reflected in their lack of predicting and monitoring activities: They do not pose questions, identify a goal, or check the extent to which answers have been confirmed. Hence, question-asking strategies appear most important for poor readers. Teachers can help readers to acquire these strategies by asking a question to get a question, by using Stauffer's group-directed reading-thinking activity (DRTA), by using the phase-out–phase-in strategy of modeling questioning behavior, and by following reciprocal questioning routines.

In addition to discussing self-generated questions, the chapter described the experience-text-relationship (ETR) method, by which readers relate their prior learning with text to produce new understanding. The chapter addressed the problem of fostering fruitful questions and selecting goals appropriate for given reading material. The development of schemata for patterns commonly used by authors was offered as one way to further communication between author and reader.

Useful Reading

Anderson, R. C., and W. B. Biddle. "On Asking People Questions About What They Are Reading." In *The Psychology of Learning and Motivation,* vol. 9, ed. G. H. Bower. New York: Academic Press, 1975.

Andre, T. "Does Answering Higher Level Questions While Reading Facilitate Productive Reading?" *Review of Educational Research* 49 (Spring 1979): 280–318.

Bransford, J. D., and M. K. Johnson. "Considerations of Some Problems of Comprehension." In *Visual Information Processing* (Proceedings of the 8th Annual Carnegie Symposium on Cognition), ed. W. G. Chase. New York: Academic Press, 1973.

Felker, D. B., and R. A. Dapra. "Effects of Question Type and Question Placement on Problem-Solving Ability from Prose Material." *Journal of Educational Psychology* 67, no. 3 (1975): 380–84.

Frase, L. T. "Purpose in Reading." In *Cognition, Curriculum and Comprehension,* ed. J. T. Guthrie. Newark, Del.: International Reading Association, 1977.

Richards, J. P. "Adjunct Post Questions in Text: A Critical Review of Methods and Processes." *Review of Educational Research* 49 (Spring 1979): 181–96.

Richards, J. P. "Interaction of Position and Conceptual Level of Adjunct Questions on Immediate and Delayed Retention of Text." *Journal of Educational Psychology* 68 (1976): 210–17.

Smith, C. "Evaluating Answers to Comprehension Questions." *Reading Teacher,* May 1978, pp. 896–900.

3 Elaboration in Reading

Overview

Comprehension can be improved by deep processing of text material. One form of deep processing is elaboration—the embellishing of what is read. Strategies for elaborating include using mental imagery, drawing inferences, notetaking, and summarizing text in one's own words. Elaboration rests on the hypothesis that when readers actively integrate new information with existing knowledge, greater storage and use of the new material will result. Although some theorists believe that elaboration works because it increases learners' interest, others attribute its effectiveness to the fact that elaboration strategies draw readers' attention to what is relevant. Still others say that elaboration is effective because it activates learners' relevant schemata, thereby allowing the new information to be incorporated into their sets of past experiences.

In this chapter you will have opportunity to learn about strategies for encouraging elaboration and to discover for yourself their value in comprehending text.

USING MENTAL IMAGERY
IN COMPREHENDING TEXT

Generally, comprehension increases when readers create images for the information they get while reading. Pressley taught eight-year-olds to construct mental pictures for the sentences and paragraphs they read.[1] Compared with a control group whose members read the story, the imagery group recalled more of the story's events. Similarly, more inferences were made by older students who were taught to create images of what was happening as they read technical text.[2] However, a few researchers report inconsistent results from attempts at imagery instruction. Jeannette Miccinate carried out an imagery program that had both auditory and visual components. She first taught pupils to draw simple stick figures representing the images generated as they listened to various passages on tape. Then pupils were asked to draw their own images as they read. This imagery training did not affect the comprehension of pupils as measured by a standardized achievement test.[3] However, it is not clear whether the tests included high-imagery sentences and passages.

Keys to effective image-making seem to lie in forming mental pictures of persons, events, or information to be learned. Readers must know the purposes of the material, its relationship to their own experiences, and the logical relationships among the ideas expressed. There may be a difference in training pupils to image *separate* sentences and in training them to generate an image that *connects* sentences. As in the case of other elaborating techniques—notetaking, outlining, underlining—successful imaging requires that the ideas singled out for attention be the important ones.

Mind's Eye is a set of procedures for helping pupils to find out what is important and to transform text into vivid mental images. The materials were developed by persons in the Escondido School District, who report that yearly average comprehension gains tripled after the technique was introduced.

The *Mind's Eye* procedure consists of these elements:[4]

1. *Key words:* Children are taught to recognize important words in sentences and passages. Initially, key words are underlined, and pupils are asked to form mental images only from these words. Later pupils

---

[1] G. M. Pressley, "Mental Imagery Helps Eight-Year Olds Remember What They Read," *Journal of Educational Psychology* 68 (1976): 355–59.

[2] R. C. Mayer, "Elaboration Techniques That Increase the Meaningfulness of Technical Text: An Experimental Test of the Learning Strategy Hypothesis," *Journal of Educational Psychology* 72 (1980): 770–84.

[3] J. Miccinate, "The Influence of a Six-Week Imagery Training Program on Children's Reading Comprehension," *Journal of Reading Behavior* 14, no. 2 (1982): 197–203.

[4] Escondido School District, *Mind's Eye* (Escondido, Calif.: Board of Education, 1979), p. 55.

automatically pick up key words and simultaneously create images for them.

2. *Discussion of images:* After silent reading of key words, pupils are asked questions that help them make clear mental pictures: "What do you see?" "Tell me about your picture." "What else can you see?" The discussion questions may also develop anticipation: "What do you think will happen next?"

3. *Oral reading:* After discussion of their mental images, pupils read orally for fluency and for verifying that their images fit the text.

Mind's Eye procedure may be used with individuals, small groups, or an entire class. The following accounts were prepared by teachers using *Mind's Eye:*

TEACHER X

Preparation

I worked with third-, fourth-, and fifth-graders for a period of two weeks to help them with visualization skills. I had them try to get different pictures for different words I would say. I used words such as *apple, rose,* or *peach.* The children were told to form a picture from these words and try to sense the feel, the touch, and the smell of the word. Thus from the word *apple,* the children would get the idea that an apple is big, round, and usually red. If you had never seen an apple, then the descriptive words would be important words; however, the word *apple* should create a mental image immediately in most of us. This way the children will spend less time trying to decode the word and spend more time making pictures as they read only a few words.

Also as part of the preparation, I told the children that they did not need to read every word in the sentence to get a picture. They only needed a few words per sentence or line to form a picture in their minds.

Procedure

I first arranged the children in a group and explained to them about *Mind's Eye.* I then showed them how to underline just a few important words per line, the ones needed to get a picture in their minds. The children underlined a few words per line and were instructed to *read only the words they underlined.* We then discussed the pictures they had in their minds and each student shared his picture. After reading several paragraphs each student then reads aloud. I had each student read some of the material—just read silently and compare oral pictures with silent pictures.

There were some words the children had to be shown to underline, such as negative words; if these words are left out, the meaning of the story is changed.

I found with my third-graders or the slower readers that they were having trouble picking out the important words. I took some of the stories that we were reading and blocked out the unimportant words. Then they read the stories with just the important words showing, and they seemed to be able to get better pictures. After we discussed the pictures they had, I then showed them the whole story and we talked about whether or not the pictures were different. They found out that their pictures were basically the same.

My fourth- and fifth-graders were able to pick up underlining much faster, and we were able to move on to the next stage. I then told them as they were reading to themselves to do the same thing as they had been doing with the pencil—only reading the important words.

Observations

I found that the younger the students were the more beginning instruction was needed. The slower readers spent more time underlining before moving on to the next stage, while the faster readers needed only to underline for a couple of days. When there was a faster reader in the group, he had to wait for the others or be allowed to continue on his own.

TEACHER Y

Setting

Begin with a group of four to six students. (Several small groups like these may be combined once the procedure has been learned.) Work with the group for a period of fifteen to twenty minutes. During this time, the rest of the class may be working at their desks.

Day One

Introduction to the Mind's Eye program—Explain to the students that when reading silently, it is not necessary to know every word in order to understand what is taking place in the story. Tell them that they are going to learn to make "pictures" or a "movie" of the stories as they read them. Discuss what is meant by important or key words—those words necessary to form a clear picture in their minds.

The story—Begin with a short story, one to two pages. Have the students underline important words in the first few sentences or first paragraph. Instruct them to form a mental image of what they are reading as they underline. Encourage them to underline as few words as necessary to make a clear picture. When all students are finished, choose one student to explain his picture to the group. When that student is through, ask if anyone has anything to add. At this point, if you notice any students who have underlined too many or not enough words, take the time to review the concept of important words and what makes them important. Continue with underlining the important words and discussing the picture for the remainder of the period. Each time the students complete their picture-telling, you may wish to choose a student to read orally the passage just discussed. Other students may follow along or close their eyes and form a picture. This procedure often helps to clarify if the students have been unable to come up with a complete or accurate picture.

Day Two

If you did not complete the story in the previous session, take a moment to briefly review what took place and recall the pictures. Do not take too much time in review. Continue with the procedure followed in Day One. It is not necessary to read orally every passage, as this sometimes impedes progress through the story and causes lack of interest. If all of the students develop an inaccurate or incomplete picture, it is helpful to ask them to scan the section for a particular point. Then ask one student to read that sentence or paragraph aloud. You should be increasing the amount read between discussions. The amount the students can read and still get good pictures will vary with each group and is left to the teacher's discretion.

Day Three

Students might be able to stop underlining and simply point to important words with a pencil or card. You will be able to tell if it is too soon for this change by the kinds of pictures the students are making. It may be necessary to go back to underlining with slower groups; however, it is encouraged that the students move away from underlining as soon as they can. This will allow them to begin working in books where they will not be able to underline. Other than this change, the same procedure as in Day One and Two should be followed.

Day Four and Beyond

If the students are making clear pictures, it may be possible to start them in a short book with short chapters. *If you do not feel they are ready, continue with the above procedure for a few more sessions.* It is not necessary that all students read the same book, but in order to get a good idea of the students' accuracy in picture making, the teacher should have read the book. Allow students to read independently, moving their own cards down the page, covering up what they have already read. They are to continue reading until they are called up for a conference. In the conference the teacher allows the student to describe his picture. Then he or she may read a section orally to the teacher.

Children benefit from being asked to make up pictures after reading an entire story. Drawing pictures to illustrate these mental images may help children process text information and relate new information to background knowledge. Generally it is better for readers to think of their own pictures than have pictures given to them. A common practice is for the teacher to give a few examples and then encourage pupils to form their own. The teacher may help pupils initially by asking them to suggest more about a central character, situation, or process than is revealed by the author. For example, after reading the sentence, *It was summer and Tony and Carla were going shopping,* pupils might be asked: "What do you think they were wearing?" "Who is taller?" Obviously, such questions call for inferences as well as mental imagery.

MAKING INFERENCES WHILE ELABORATING

The poorest performance on tests involving reading is elicited by items that demand inference—the deriving of some idea that is not directly stated. John Carroll has suggested three ways for deriving inferences from

Activity 3.1   Assessing the Value of Visual Imagery

General Procedures

1.   Select a passage (paragraph, story, article) that you would like your pupils to know about. The passage should be unfamiliar to the pupils. Try to select a passage that you think gives rise to imagery.
2.   Randomly divide your class into two groups (assigning every other name in the roll book to the same group works well).
3.   Read the entire passage to both groups. Then ask members of one group to draw simple pictures depicting the event described in the passage. Members of the other group may draw pictures of something they like a lot.
4.   Collect the pictures and note whether those who illustrated the passage depicted accurate and relevant information or not. Did they relate ideas expressed in the passage?
5.   Several days later, ask members of both groups to write a summary of the passage.
6.   Score the summaries on the basis of number of central ideas and events recalled.
7.   Average and compare the scores earned by the two groups.

Analyzing the Results

According to cognitive theory, the overall performance of the group that drew pictures depicting the ideas and events of the passage should be better than that of the group that drew unrelated pictures. The construction of the image is supposed to help the reader integrate and remember the text. Perhaps the results will not be so clear for children younger than eight years old. Some children below this age have difficulty in generating images when instructed to do so.

You should examine the results to see if children thought to be poor readers did as well with the imagery condition as good readers did without it. When analyzing your data, you may wish to include in your imagery group averages only the scores for persons who were able to depict accurate and relevant images.

passages.[5] A reader can infer meaning from the subtleties of verbal expression: *She was a viscountess, but he was only a baron.* Even if you do not know the ranks of the British peerage, you can tell that viscountesses are higher in rank than barons. How? By linguistic awareness of the word *only.*

[5] John B. Carroll, "From Comprehension to Inference," *33rd Yearbook, Claremont Reading Conference,* ed. Malcolm Douglas (Claremont, Calif.: Claremont Graduate School, 1969).

Similarly, Roger Shank's favorite example of how people make inferences involves the word *but*. He thinks the word *but* basically means "call off the inference." If you say "I ate dinner but I'm still hungry," the *but* says that the usual inference—that you are satisfied after eating—isn't true in this case.[6]

In other instances a reader derives inferences through reasoning. *Bill isn't as tall as Mary but he's much taller than Steve.* Who is the tallest? A third way inferences are made involves the reader's using personal experience to infer how characters in text might feel:

> The delight that Tad had felt during his long hours in the glen faded as he drew near the cabin. The sun was nearly gone and Tad's father was at the woodpile. He was wearing his broadcloth suit that he wore to church and to town sometimes. He was doing Tad's work and in his good clothes. Tad ran to him. "I'll get it, Pa."

When Tad saw his father, did he feel (a) disappointed, (b) important, (c) angry, (d) guilty? To infer that Tad felt guilty, the reader must not only understand the surface level of the paragraph but apprehend the total situation.

Schema theory addresses the question of how we apprehend the deeper facts and relationships that lurk in text. This theory posits that most of what we read represents a stereotyped sequence of actions or events. Our familiarity with the schema allows us to infer the appropriate connections.[7] *John knew his wife's operation would be very expensive. There was always Uncle Henry. He reached for the phone book.* Comprehension of this passage may rest on a "raising money for important expenditures" schema evoked by the words.

In addition to helping readers infer omitted details, a schema helps them elaborate the text. That is, readers may generate thoughts consistent with the schema invoked but not necessarily supported in any way by the text. In the above example, inferences might be made about how the couple felt about each other and about the nature of the operation; many other elaborations might be based on the reader's own experience with such situations.

Elaborations from inference serve important functions. They help us find connections among sentences; they generate expectations about subsequent information; and they aid retention. To illustrate the inferences children must make when reading, consider this paragraph and then answer the question that follows:

> The Benchley family was out riding with their German Shepherd. After they pulled on to the shoulder to change drivers, young Marie slipped and broke

[6] "A Conversation with Roger Shank," *Psychology Today* 17 (April 1983): 28–36.
[7] L. M. Reder, "The Role of Elaboration in the Comprehension and Retention of Prose: A Critical Review," *Review of Educational Research* 50 (Spring 1980): 5–53.

her ankle. They raced to the hospital and were getting out of the car when they noticed that Shep was missing.

What happened to Shep? If you answered the question at all, you did as well as a kindergarten child of whom John Guthrie asked this question.[8] If you could provide details of how Shep got lost, you performed as well as two third-graders and one fifth-grader.

The question and answer seem simple, but the necessary inferences are substantial. Here are some of them: Benchleys had (probably owned) a dog that they cared about. Everyone in the family was healthy and happy. They were riding down the highway in a car and decided to change drivers, which required stopping the car. Two people got out of the car; both walked around it and got back in. While the car was stopped, the doors were opened. Marie got out and slipped hard enough to break an ankle. After they discovered that she had broken her ankle, the Benchleys hurried to a hospital. Getting to a hospital fast is important. Hurried people close doors quickly. In normal circumstances, attention is broadly deployed. When there is no threat, injury, or unbalance in their equilibrium, people attend to many different happenings. When a problem occurs, however, attention is focused on it. Also, people are more important than dogs; an injury is especially important, and an injured person commands more attention than a healthy dog. In an accident, the Benchleys paid close attention to the injured person. As the problem was partly solved by getting to the hospital, attention was broadened to include Shep and to note that he was missing.

The process of elaborating aids long-term retention. If passages are richly elaborated during reading, then only a few statements need be retrieved for the gist of the original text to be recalled. If teachers provide pupils with information that makes it easier to elaborate a given text, pupils will remember more about it.

One major difference between poor readers and good readers is the speed with which they make inferences and elaborate. Recommendations for improving their speed include the following:

1. Make sure that children are aware that there is a difference between the literal meaning of a text and the deeper meaning that is found in the inferences drawn from it. Although children constantly draw inferences in real life, they don't seem to realize fully the need for drawing inferences from their reading. Many readers spend much time looking for a directly stated answer in the text when the answer to the question must be inferred.
2. Illustrate the drawing of inferences over and over again, using a variety of textual materials—literature, newspaper stories, editorials.

---

[8] John Guthrie, "Purpose and Text Structure," *Reading Teacher* 32 (February 1979): 624–26.

With repeated exposure to situations, the reader develops stereotyped generalizations that allow formation of a well-constructed
causal chain to predict behavior.
3. Give children much practice in drawing inferences so they can automatically infer the important information necessary for comprehending what follows in a text.

Jane Hansen has shown us an interesting way to help children draw
inferences from their reading.[9] Hansen's strategy and questioning procedure enhanced the ability of children to answer comprehension questions
about the story selection she used. Hansen offered no conclusive evidence that the procedures resulted in pupils' spontaneously applying the
strategy in reading unfamiliar stories. However, her procedures have
been combined and tried with good and poor readers and in other contexts; the results suggest that inferential instruction may be especially
well suited for poor readers.

A PROCEDURE FOR HELPING PUPILS INFER

The intent of inference training lessons is to make pupils aware of the
importance of drawing inferences to link new information with their existing knowledge. To this end, the teacher identifies one or more key ideas
implicit in the selection to be read. This idea becomes the basis for discussion prior to reading—a discussion in which children have the opportunity to report their experience with the idea. Often, the idea is presented
in the form of a problem or story. The discussion activates schemata for
children to use in making inferences as they read. More than that, the
knowledge recalled is used to make predictions about what might happen
in the story. Pupils hypothesize about what the protagonist will do in a
situation similar to one they themselves have experienced. Next, the
children read the selection and then engage in another discussion in which
they answer inferential questions suggested by the text. The following
illustration involves a lesson in which the pupils are to read Ouida Sebestyen's *IOU'S*.[10]

Key Idea
Before having students read the book *IOU'S,* the teacher identifies two
themes: (a) the possibility that a child may have a teasing, affectionate
relationship with a parent rather than see parents as adversarial authorities and (b) the way people may dam up their feelings to avoid losing
someone's approval and to keep things as they are.

[9] Jane Hansen, "The Effect of Inference Training and Practice on Young Children's Reading
Comprehension," *Reading Research Quarterly* 16 (1981): 391–417.
[10] Ouida Sebestyen, *IOU'S* (Boston: Little, Brown, 1982).

I. *Prereading Discussion*
    a. *Purpose*
        Pupils know the purpose for the prereading discussion and
        remind themselves of what they are doing and why. "Before
        we read, we talk about our lives—those parts that relate to
        what the story is about." "We also predict what will happen
        in the story." "We compare our experiences with what takes
        place, so that we will better understand the story."
    b. *Questions for Activating Background Experiences*
        "Have you ever had a friend whose relationship with parents
        is different from your relationship with your parents?" "How
        was it different?" "In the story that we will read, Stowie's
        friend Brownie questions the way Stowie acts toward his
        mother—and his need for his mother's approval."
    c. *Hypothesis*
        "On the basis of your own experiences, do you think Stowie
        will pursue his own way even if it isn't what his mother
        thinks?" "Will his mother help Stowie expose himself to the
        fear of losing her affection?"
II. *Postreading Questions*
    "Why did Stowie not tell his mother that his grandfather was ill?"
    "Did Stowie mean it when he said, 'Let me be better to her than
    they were; I want to make it up to my mother'?"
    Similar formats can be followed for expository material. For exam-
    ple, in introducing factual material about three-dimensional shapes, the
    teacher might activate pupils' backgrounds by drawing approximations of
    the shapes—sphere, hemisphere, cube, cylinder, cone—on the chalk-
    board and asking "Of what does each of these shapes remind you?"
    Prediction would follow, and the teacher might make such comments as,
    "In this chapter you will learn how many sides each shape has and what
    the sides look like. On the basis of your experience with cylinders, will
    the cross-section be circular? What will the sides be? What shape will the
    longitudinal section be?"

OTHER WAYS TO ELABORATE TEXT

Merl Wittrock has written extensively on the importance of generative
activities that lead pupils to construct relations among the parts of the text
and between the text and their personal knowledge and experience. In
one of his studies, 400 sixth-graders were asked to write in their own words
a sentence about each of several paragraphs immediately after reading it.
In addition, some groups of children were given paragraph headings,
either to be incorporated into their sentences or omitted from them. The
generation of their own sentences was expected to facilitate the students'

construction of relationships among experience, knowledge, and the text. The paragraph headings were intended to serve as cues for relevant schemata. Results of the study show that a combination of sentence generation and use of headings was most effective in enhancing retention and comprehension, followed by sentence generation and then use of headings. The use of paragraph headings was more effective with the better readers, while the sentence generation was better with the poorer readers. The combination of the two methods doubled comprehension for children of various levels of reading ability.[11]

It appears that elaboration requires the learner to create a construction that when combined with new information, gives this information more meaning. Underlining, notetaking, and categorizing are important ways to induce elaborations. This is so at least when the reader is able to identify the main ideas by underlining or otherwise singling out. Rewriting parts of a selection in order to produce different conclusions, giving analogies, providing examples, and writing summaries are other valuable activities that enhance elaboration and comprehension. Similarly, teachers can ask pupils to identify those parts of a selection that are of personal significance by asking: "What important points have been left out?" "Why are these points important?" "What would happen if people did what the author suggests?" "Before we read the story, you told me _____; now what do you think about _____?"

Asking pupils questions *after* reading will help them retain both the information that answers the questions and other information addressed while reading the text. Applying information and ideas gained from reading to other situations is a powerful means of elaboration. Providing opportunities for pupils to relate reading to writings, drama, and discussions is valuable; and encouraging them to use the new content in out-of-school situations, such as reading to the blind and sharing their new knowledge with fathers and mothers, is an effective learning strategy.

In brief, elaboration—relating material to previous knowledge (directly or by analogy) and creating logical relationships among components of the material (as in summarizing)—makes new information meaningful.

GOING BEYOND THE AUTHOR'S INTENTIONS

Traditional testing in reading usually assumes there is a single right answer to each question. In contrast, an interactive view of reading holds the possibility that other answers may be acceptable, inasmuch as mean-

[11] M. C. Wittrock, C. B. Marks, and M. J. Doctorow, "Reading as a Generative Process," *Journal of Educational Psychology* 67 (1975): 484–89.

ing is always a mediation between the worlds of the author and the reader. The reader makes an assessment of the text as a whole using the perspective available to him or her. Yet, collision with the material itself may influence the reader's preconceptions, resulting in what someone once termed "a fusion of horizons." If you accept the idea that meaning is not only to be found in the text but in interaction between the text and the reader, then you are obligated to find out how the child is interpreting the text. A child's answer is not an error just because it does not match someone else's expectations.

What children bring to their reading by way of elaboration is wondrous. Different people may use different logic to connect the same two events. John Guthrie tells about hearing two fifth-graders discussing a story about Robert Frost.[12] Frost was working as a farmer and seemed to be thoroughly enjoying himself by endlessly fiddling around with words. One child said that Frost's fiddling was understandable because Frost was seeking self-expression. The other child said that he did not think that fiddling with words was strange since Frost would probably write some good poems and sell them for a lot of money. These children had distinct but logical ways of interpreting Frost's fiddling with words.

Idiosyncratic responses to text can be dealt with in several ways:

1. Accept initially the child's statement about the text and then explore with the child the ramifications of the statement. In the process, the statement may be modified by the child.
2. Accept an emotional reaction to the text, but have the child examine the assumptions underlying the reaction.
3. Teach the child procedures to better understand what the writer was trying to say. By way of example, Alan Purves offers a schema by which one can derive meaning from a literary work.[13] The schema consists of seven heuristics (problem-solving strategies) for deriving the theme for a difficult text—*The Heart of Darkness:* (a) assume the importance of Marlowe and look at all his generalizations; (b) assume the importance of the title and examine the use of *heart* and *darkness;* (c) look for juxtaposition and stated or implied comparisons; (d) look for repetitions of word or event; (e) look at the motif of the story and for analogies in other journeys; (f) look at the structure of the story— the frame tale—and seek to determine the relationship of frame to tale; (g) explain a particular character and see if he or she embodies a theme.

---

[12] John Guthrie, "Purpose and Text Structure," *Reading Teacher* 32 (February 1979).
[13] Alan Purves, *Putting Readers in Their Places: Some Alternatives to Cloning Stanley Fish,* ERIC Document ED 179974, 1979.

Activity 3.2 Deriving Meaning from Print—Individual Variations

Are you entitled to read into a poem or other text material anything you choose? While no two people respond in exactly the same way and while one person may see deeper meanings in a text than another, we should be able to support what we get out of a text by reference to what it actually says.

By looking very closely at what authors literally say and the way they say it, you may perceive meanings, fully supported by the texts, that the authors themselves have not seen. However, in making your own meaning, you have to stick to what is on the page.

This activity is designed to illustrate the idea that individuals derive different meanings from the same text material, to give you an opportunity to practice dealing with differences in interpretation, and to explain these differences in terms of individual schemata.

General procedures

1.   Read William Wordsworth's *The World*. Pay regard to (a) the main idea of the poem; (b) the attitude toward nature; (c) the attitude toward humankind; (d) the form, language, and manner of expression; and (e) the relevancy of the poem to your own condition.

The World
The world is too much with us; late and soon,
   Getting and spending, we lay waste our powers:
Little we see in Nature that is ours;
We have given our hearts away, a sordid boon!
This Sea that bares her bosom to the moon;
   The winds that will be howling at all hours,
   And are up-gather'd now like sleeping flowers;
For this, for everything, we are out of tune;
It moves us not.—Great God! I'd rather be
   A Pagan suckled in a creed outworn;
So might I, standing on this pleasant lea,
   Have glimpses that would make me less forlorn;
Have sight of Proteus rising from the sea;
   Or hear old Triton blow his wreathed horn.

2.   Compare your response with those of your colleagues. What concepts and inferences account for your differences in interpretation? Did you or your colleagues use any of Purves's seven heuristics in determining the main ideas? Which did you use? Was each person's interpretation supported by the text? Do some persons have literary schemata that enabled them to gain more meaning from the poem than others? Describe some of these schemata.

SUMMARY

Elaboration is especially important *while* reading, although—in the form of orienting instructions, priming questions, and summaries—it can be applied *before* and *after* reading. The more elaborations generated, the greater the recall of what is read. The amount of elaboration can be influenced by instructions—the giving of background information, the encouraging of imagery, and the preparation of summaries. Relevant background knowledge is a prerequisite to drawing the required inferences, and inferences and elaborations made during reading should relate to what is to be remembered. Elaboration should focus upon critical statements in a text, not upon unimportant ones. Readers who learn to automatically draw inferences and elaborate upon key aspects of text will greatly improve in their comprehension.

Useful Reading

Doctorow, M. J., M. C. Wittrock, and C. B. Marks. "Generative Processes in Reading Comprehension." *Journal of Educational Psychology* 70 (1978): 109–18.

Highest, K. L. "Recent Research on Visual Mnemonics." *Review of Educational Research* 9 (Fall 1979): 611–29.

Paris, S. G., B. K. Lindauer, and G. L. Cox. "The Development of Inferential Comprehension." *Child Development* 48 (1977): 1728–33.

Peper, K. J., and R. E. Mager. "Notetaking as a Generative Activity." *Journal of Educational Psychology* 70 (1978): 514–22.

Pressley, G. M. "Imagery and Children's Learning: Putting the Picture in Developmental Perspective." *Review of Educational Research* 47 (Fall 1977): 585–622.

Reder, L. M. "The Role of Elaboration in the Comprehension and Retention of Prose: A Critical Review." *Review of Educational Research* 50 (Spring 1980): 5–53.

Schank, R. C., and R. P. Abelson. *Scripts, Plans, Goals, and Understanding: An Inquiry into Human Knowledge Structures.* Hillsdale, N.J.: Erlbaum, 1977.

Trabasso, T. "On the Making of Inferences During Reading and Their Assessment." Technical Report no. 157. Urbana: Center for the Study of Reading, University of Illinois, January 1980.

Wittrock, M. C. "Learning as a Generative Process." *Educational Psychologist* 11 (1974): 87–95.

4 Restructuring Schemata

IDENTIFYING CONFLICTING COGNITIVE STRUCTURES

FORMING AND CHANGING SCHEMATA
    Accretion and Fine-Tuning
    Restructuring

MODELS FOR RESTRUCTURING SCHEMATA
    The Dialectical Model for Restructuring Schemata
    The Inquiry Method for Restructuring Schemata
    Communication Theory and the Restructuring of
      Schemata

SUMMARY

Overview

Thus far this book has emphasized schema theory as it contributes to
assimilation, by which new information from reading is fitted into
existing schemata, or "new wine is placed in old bottles." Now we
consider *accommodation,* or the restructuring of general schemata,
which provides new bottles, not just wine.

    Assimilation in reading demands that the reader interpret
something using an existing schema, answering such questions as:
"How does this add to what I already know?" On the other hand,
accommodation demands suspending judgment, or withholding
interpretation. Accommodation implies the possibility that the reader's
schemata may shift. It requires answering such questions as: "What is
the author's perspective?" "What evidence does the author offer for
the new propositions?" "Do the new propositions address my
fundamental concerns better than my present way of thinking and
acting?"

    Pupils come to school both with schemata acquired from many
cultural sources—TV, parents, friends—and with the capacity to be

58

involved in what they read. Sometimes the schemata based on the pupils' everyday experience of the world conflict with the concepts met in reading. Thus the teacher is faced not with a problem of helping the student absorb new information but with a problem of modifying the whole or large parts of the student's cognitive structure.

When there are discrepancies between the knowledge structures of the readers and reality as perceived by the author, the readers either fail to learn, forget what they have read (but only after they have completed the examination on the material, of course), or unknowingly misinterpret what they have read so that the new information is not in conflict with their earlier ideas. In this chapter, emphasis is placed upon readers' viewpoints and, where appropriate, upon procedures to modify them.

IDENTIFYING CONFLICTING COGNITIVE STRUCTURES

Roger Osborne and John Gilbert explored the scientific understandings of students that differ from scientists' viewpoints.[1] They found that students often hold incongruous beliefs. For example, when asked about the force on a person in a satellite, many students, even some as old as nineteen, said there was no air in space and, therefore, no gravity. The knowledge structures of students are frequently not the structures authors and teachers assume students have. Readers' views of the world and meanings for words are not isolated ideas but conceptual structures by which the readers make sense of their lives. The more teachers know about and appreciate the cognitive structures of their students, the more they will be able to provide learning opportunities for modifying the structures.

I have found in my own classes that teachers' preexisting frameworks about reading are highly resistant to extinction despite instruction. Further, the conflicting frameworks play a crucial interfering role in learning about the teaching of reading. You can test this for yourself. In the activity to follow, there are three parts—a listing of five ideologies regarding the proper goal of reading; brief passages describing theories of how readers best learn to read; and a short posttest. In completing this activity, note how your conceptual view of the purpose of reading affects the meaning you derive from the passages on theory. These passages, interesting reading in their own right, have been adapted from an article by Peter Mosenthal.[2]

---

[1] Roger Osborne and John Gilbert, "A Technique for Exploring Students' Views of the World," *Journal of Physics Education* 15 (1980): 376–79.
[2] Peter Mosenthal, "Designing Training Programs for Learning Disabled Children: An Ideological Perspective," *Topics in Learning and Learning Disabilities* 2, no. 1 (1982): 97–106.

Activity 4.1   Do Preconceptions Affect Ability to Learn from Text?

As indicated in the text, this activity includes three sets of materials—a set of goal statements, some passages to read, and a posttest. Please don't look at the posttest until directed.

There are three steps to the activity: first, select the goal statement that is *least* like your concept of the goal for reading; second, read the passages about theories of reading; and third, take the posttest and note the parts of the test on which you do best. You can then see whether or not you learned less from the passages that conflict with your conception of reading goals than from the passages consistent with your predispositions.

1. *Goal Statements*

   Put a mark by the goal statement *least* like your own view.

   _____ a. *Cognitive development.* The goal of reading is to promote intellectual growth—to enhance the reader's ability to use a variety of strategies on a variety of tasks and types of content. Students should learn strategies for processing information efficiently.

   _____ b. *Emancipation.* The goal of reading is to change the social and political structure so that the oppressed may forge a new, more just relationship with their oppressors. Reading teachers should hold high expectations for learners, sensitizing them to their social situation and allowing them to be literate in the areas most likely to improve their social condition.

   _____ c. *Romanticism.* The goal of reading is to develop an individual's autonomy and self-worth. Reading should focus on the development of self-knowledge by offering a broad range of experiences to increase knowledge.

   _____ d. *Utility.* The goal is to teach students survival skills in a complex technological society. They should learn to read the kinds of materials they will encounter in real life—application forms, contracts, safety instructions. Reading of real-world materials should be stressed.

   _____ e. *Academic achievement.* The goal is to pass on the knowledge, skills, and social values of the culture that have been prized by great scholars. Students should learn to reproduce facts and ideas from text. The meanings derived should be those deemed correct by an authority.

2. *Reading Theories*

   Read the following passages regarding theories of reading. In the passages the following technical terms appear:

   Reproduction—literal meaning of a text.

   Reconstruction—permissible interpretation of a text.

   Embellishment—meaning independent of the text.

Activity 4.1   *(Continued)*

a. *Levels-of-Processing Theories*

Levels-of-processing theories focus on the task. Good learning is defined as the ability to correctly apply a meaning process to a given meaning source. Failure to correctly perform a task is explainable in terms of the inability to comprehend the task and thus the inability to meet its performance criterion.

These theories presuppose two meaning sources—meaning in prior text and meaning in current text—and two meaning processes—reproduction and reconstruction. The theories are therefore limited in that they fail to deal with meaning in the social situation or meaning in prior knowledge; in addition, they fail to deal with creative meaning.

b. *Metamemory Theories*

Metamemory theories focus on the interaction of the materials, the task, and the learner. Most metamemory theories define good learning as (1) the ability to monitor incoming information against some sensible set of criteria and (2) the ability to be flexible in adjusting processing strategies, where necessary, so that the criteria for comprehending are met. In metamemory theories, failure to learn can be explained in terms of several factors: (1) the inability to adequately assess what is known, (2) the inability to establish adequate criteria for monitoring incoming information, and (3) the inability to establish or change monitoring strategies so that criteria for learning can be met.

In general, metamemory theories presuppose several meaning sources—meaning in prior knowledge and meaning in prior text, in current text, and in future text—and several meaning processes—reproduction, reconstruction, and embellishment. These theories are more inclusive than the theories discussed earlier. They are limited, however, in that they fail to deal with the influences of the situation organizer and of the setting contexts and thus fail to consider meaning in social interaction.

c. *Schema Theories*

Schema theories focus principally on the learner. In schema theories, good learning is defined as the ability to correctly realize new information in terms of prior information—that is, to *instantiate* new information. Failure is explained in terms of either a lack of background knowledge or an inability to correctly instantiate incoming information in terms of the appropriate cognitive categories.

Schema theories presuppose one source of meaning—meaning in prior knowledge—and two meaning processes—reconstruction and embellishment. Thus these theories are limited in that they deal primarily with how pupils comprehend pragmatic inference and creative meaning.

Activity 4.1 *(Continued)*

d. *Behavioristic and Hulleanistic Theories*

Behavioristic and Hulleanistic theories focus mostly on the materials and somewhat on the learner. In these theories, good learning is defined as the ability to correctly match a response with a given stimulus. Failure is generally explained in terms of the incapacity to mediate information so that a correct response is automatically matched with a corresponding stimulus. In addition, failure is explained in terms of stimulus complexity.

These theories presuppose one source of meaning—meaning in current text—and one meaning process—reproduction. Thus, the theories are limited in that they deal only with how children learn to comprehend referential meaning.

e. *Classroom Competence Theories*

Classroom competence theories focus on the interaction of the task, the situation, the learner, and the materials. General classroom competence models argue that teachers perceive children in their classrooms as having different competencies. These perceptions result in different expectations, thus influencing how teachers interact with children. These interactions in turn produce varying performance among children.

In addition, because children have different social expectations, they have different notions of what constitutes appropriate classroom behavior in interacting with teachers. Thus children have different ideas about when, where, and with whom they should speak and act. Classroom competence models further postulate that how children perceive the risk and ambiguity in their interactions influences their selection of meaning sources and meaning processes.

In classroom competence theories, failure to learn can be explained in terms of failure to negotiate the appropriate use of meaning in interacting with a teacher, task, and set of materials or in terms of teachers' having low expectations of certain children's performance.

Classroom competence theories presuppose several meaning sources—meaning in prior knowledge, meaning in prior text, meaning in current text, and meaning in social interaction—and several meaning processes—reproduction, reconstruction, and embellishment. Such theories tend to include more meaning sources and meaning processes than even metamemory theories. They are limited, however, in that they fail to consider meaning in future text and ignore the question of how different aspects of the setting context influence comprehension and integration of meaning in memory.

Activity 4.1   (*Continued*)

---

3. *Posttest*
   a. Name the meaning processes associated with each of the
      following theories.
      1. Competence _____
      2. Levels-of-processing _____
      3. Schema _____
      4. Metamemory _____
      5. Behavioristic _____
   b. Name the meaning sources associated with each of the following
      theories.
      1. Behavioristic _____
      2. Metamemory _____
      3. Schema _____
      4. Levels-of-processing _____
      5. Competence _____

   Answers
   a. 1. Reproduction, reconstruction, embellishment.
      2. Reproduction, reconstruction.
      3. Reconstruction, embellishment.
      4. Reproduction, reconstruction, embellishment.
      5. Reproduction.
   b. 1. Current text.
      2. Prior knowledge, prior text, current text, future text.
      3. Prior knowledge.
      4. Prior knowledge, current text.
      5. Prior knowledge, prior text, social interaction.

4. *Interpretation of Responses*
   Your recall of answers should have matched your goal orientation.
You should have had more difficulty in recalling information about the
theory that was *least* like your conception.

Goal orientation	Matching theory
Cognitive development	Metamemory
Academic achievement	Behavioristic and Hulleanistic
Utility	Levels-of-processing
Romanticism	Schema
Emancipation	Classroom competence

Thus, for example, if you were in conflict with the emancipation
viewpoint, you would be expected to have recalled less well key
information from your reading about classroom competency theories.

FORMING AND CHANGING SCHEMATA

There are three views of how schemata are formed and changed. Exhibit 4.1 outlines a classification of these views proposed by David Rumelhart and Donald Norman.

Exhibit 4.1   The Acquisition of Schemata as Learning Tasks

Accretion	*Learning Restructuring*	*Fine-Tuning*
Matching new information with previously available schemata; adding to the data base of knowledge when it corresponds with existing schemata	Restructuring existing schemata when new information does not fit currently available schemata or when the organization of existing data structures is not satisfactory	Adjusting to terms to improve accuracy, improve generalizability, improve specificity, and make inferences from text

---

Source: Classification suggested by David Rumelhart and Donald Norman, *Accretion, Tuning, Restructuring: Three Modes of Learning,* Report 7602 (La Jolla, Calif.: La Jolla Center for Human Information Processing, August 1976), p. 26.

Accretion and Fine-Tuning

Much of our present teaching practice is based on the notion that schemata are usually developed by *accretion* and *fine-tuning* or assimilation. Accretion is merely putting new information into a schema we already have. When you read a newspaper account of an election, you probably fill your election slot with information about who won and which issues were favored. However, your basic schema for elections doesn't change much. Fine-tuning refers to changing the categories we use in interpreting new information. It involves minor modifications in existing schemata. In fine-tuning, irrelevant aspects of a schema are dropped and new variables are added. Examples include the little child who learns that not all animals are "doggies" and the person who modifies his schema of an automobile after seeing a car with only three wheels. Teachers engage pupils in tuning by sharing a broad experience with them, asking them to list the components of the experience, categorizing and labeling the components, and discovering the reasons why only members of each category belong.

Restructuring

Restructuring is a major change in an individual's schema system. Usually it occurs when the person's broad perspectives are remodeled—when he or she comes to see things very differently. A shift in a politician's views from conservative to liberal is an example. Richard Anderson has speculated on how large shifts in perspective—such as religious and political conversions—occur.[3] He believes that a teacher's critical questions can cause a person to modify world views, ideologies, and theories.

Through questioning, pupils come to recognize differences between their currently held schemata and alternatives; questioning may lead pupils to appraise the power of an alternative. To the extent that pupils engage in critical discourse, they open themselves to persuasion.

Teachers from primary school to graduate school enjoin their students to be open-minded, to honor consistent arguments, and then weigh evidence. Thus, it would be surprising if prose did not sometimes effect a change in mind.

Summaries of social-psychological research, on the other hand, indicate that it is likely that new information will be resisted if its acceptance requires major cognitive reorganization.

We resist new information when it requires that we change a large number of other logically related beliefs in order to maintain consistency among them. Resistance to a new schema takes the form of counterarguing with the learner's current framework, treating anomalies as exceptions that prove the rule, and keeping incompatible schemata separate.

Pupils' schemata are not reconstructed merely by the laying on of a new set of propositions. You have known pupils who appear to have changed their ideas when in fact they have merely assimilated the information into old schemata. "Playing the game of school" is recognized as meeting surface expectations for tests and the classroom but holding fast to schemata from out-of-school experiences that conflict with the classroom view. Faced with propositions from teachers and texts that are not in keeping with their own conceptual frameworks, pupils have to either modify their views or keep the new schemata separate from existing generalizations.

The problem of restructuring is particularly acute in schools where tension is created between individual and family views and the views of a larger society. In confronting some types of cognitive conflict, pupils cannot simply adopt new schemata or even consider what is true or accu-

[3] R. C. Anderson, "The Notion of Schemata and the Educational Enterprise," in *Schooling and the Acquisition of Knowledge,* ed. R. C. Anderson, R. J. Spiro, and W. E. Montague (Hillsdale, N.J.: Erlbaum, 1977).

rate because acceptance of the newer views would have too severe personal and social consequences.

In his moving autobiography, Richard Rodriguez, the son of poor Mexican immigrants, tells how, in order to succeed academically, he had to move from the environment of the home to the environment of the classroom, at the opposite cultural extremes.[4] Without extraordinary determination and the influence of others—at home and at school—there is little chance poor minority children will advance in academic studies. Rodriguez found that his academic success distanced him from a life he loved, even from his own memory of self. Initially, he waivered, balanced allegiances, using much of both home and school. Gradually, the balance was lost. Rodriguez needed to spend more time in the world of the school. As he advanced in his studies, his parents became figures of lost authority. He grew embarrassed by their lack of education and, to evade nostalgia, concentrated on the benefits education would bestow. A primary reason for his success in the classroom was that he allowed schooling to change him and to separate him from the life he had enjoyed before becoming a student. The school bid him to trust reason, while parents had taught him to trust spontaneity and nonrational ways of knowing. The allegiance Rodriguez might have given his mother and father was transferred to his teachers.

> I began by imitating their accents, using their diction, trusting their every direction. The very first facts they dispensed I grasped with awe. Any book they told me to read, I read—then waited for them to tell me which books I enjoyed. Their every casual opinion I came to adopt and to trumpet when I returned home.[5]

In an early grade Rodriguez was baffled by the isolation reading required. He felt lonely when reading. Only after a teacher playfully ran through complex sentences, calling the words alive with her voice, making it seem that the author somehow was speaking directly at him, did he sense the possibility of fellowship between a reader and a writer—not intimate like the words spoken at home, but nonetheless personal.

In the upper grades, Rodriguez read a great deal and had favorite writers. But often the writers he enjoyed the most he was least able to value. Reading helped him sense something of the major concerns of Western thought and brought him academic success. But he wasn't a good reader—merely bookish. He lacked a point of view when he read. Rather, he read in order to get a point of view.

For Rodriguez, education required radical self-reformation; his story centers on how great is the change any academic undergoes as well as

---

[4] Richard Rodriguez, *Hunger of Memory: The Education of Richard Rodriguez* (Boston: David R. Godine, 1981).

[5] Rodriguez, *Hunger of Memory*, p. 49.

how far one student had to move from his past. For him, education was a long, unglorious, even demeaning process—until he came to trust the silence of reading and the habit of abstracting from immediate experience. It was education in the end that allowed him to confront his desire for the past and to speak and care about that fact.

MODELS FOR RESTRUCTURING SCHEMATA

Teaching models that have demonstrated effectiveness for restructuring schemata are hard to find. However, approaches involving the deliberate creating of cognitive dissonance are promising. (Cognitive dissonance occurs when the pupil feels dissatisfied upon experiencing disequilibrium in ideas and must reduce the dissonance, incongruity, or conflict between the opposing schemata.) Promising, too, are methods involving analyzing a text and reading a given text from different perspectives. Communication theory that emphasizes the importance of perceiving the writer as truthful and that stipulates the conditions necessary for accepting the views of others provides a fresh direction to the teaching of reading.

The Dialectical Model for Restructuring Schemata

Allan Collins offers a dialectical model in which the teacher plays devil's advocate, applying a strategy to counter the pupil's resistance to arguments and evidence (resistance that results from conflict with currently held schemata).[6] Some of the rules in Collins's strategy are as follows:

1. Bring out any facts the student knows about the issue.
2. Determine what causal factors the student knows.
3. Determine if the student knows how causal factors are related.
4. Help the student determine which factors are insufficient.
5. Give the student a counter-example for an insufficient one—"Why doesn't the cause hold good in this case?"
6. If the student overlooks a fact, ask why the factor does not apply.
7. Pose a misleading question in order to free the student to learn about exceptions to the general rule.
8. Ask for a prediction about an unknown case.
9. Ask for consideration of other factors.

[6] Allan Collins, "Processes in Acquiring Knowledge," in *Schooling and the Acquisition of Knowledge,* ed. R. C. Anderson, R. J. Spiro, and W. E. Montague (Hillsdale, N.J.: Erlbaum, 1977).

The following "Fragments of a Dialogue on Growing Grain" is an illustration of the strategy used by Collins.[7]

1. T: Where in North America do you think rice might be grown? (Rule 1: Ask about a known case.)
2. S: Louisiana.
3. T: Why there? (Rule 2: Ask for any factors.)
4. S: Places where there is a lot of water. I think rice requires the ability to selectively flood fields.
5. T: OK. Do you think there's a lot of rice in, say, Washington and Oregon? (Rule 5: Pick a counter-example for an insufficient factor.)
6. S: Aha, I don't think so.
7. T: Why? (Rule 2: Ask for any factors.)
8. S: There's a lot of water up there too, but there's two reasons. First the climate isn't conducive, and second, I don't think the land is flat enough. You've got to have flat land so you can flood a lot of it, unless you terrace it.
9. T: How about Japan? (Rule 5: Pick a counter-example for an unnecessary factor.)
10. S: Yeah, well they have this elaborate technology I suppose for terracing land so they can flood it selectively even though it's tilted overall.
11. T: Do you think they might grow rice in Florida? (Rule 8: Ask for a prediction about an unknown case.)
12. S: Yeah, I guess they could, if there were an adequate fresh water supply. Certainly a nice, big, flat area.
13. T: What kind of grains do you think they grow in Africa, and where, then? (Pause) Well, where would they grow rice if they grew it anywhere? (Rule 8: Ask for a prediction about an unknown case.)
14. S: If they grew it anywhere, I suppose they'd grow it in the Nile region, and they'd grow it in the tropics where there was an adequate terrain for it.
15. T: What do you think they live on (in West Africa) (Rule 8: Ask for a prediction about an unknown case.)
16. S: I guess they grow some kind of grain in West Africa.
17. T: What kind is most likely?
18. S: Wheat.
19. T: You think wheat is the most likely grain?
20. S: Wheat or some combination of wheat and rice if they can grow it, and I suppose they could. I don't really know much about the geography there, but I suppose there are places, like Nigeria is pretty fertile.

[7] Collins, "Processes in Acquiring Knowledge," pp. 351–52.

21. T: OK. It's fertile but what are its other qualities? Is the temperature warm or cold? (Rule 9: Ask for consideration of different factors.)
22. S: Yeah, the climate's temperature and . . .
23. T: Do they have rain or not? (Rule 9: Ask for consideration of different factors.)
24. S: Yeah.
25. T: They have a lot of rain. OK. What do kinds of configurations predict as far as grain goes? (Rule 8: Ask for a prediction about an unknown case.)
26. S: Rice.

Note how Collins's strategy forces students to deal with counter-examples and face contradictions. Note, too, how it is the student who is constructing the new schema, instead of being handed the teacher's schema. The teacher keeps the pupils working until they have constructed a framework that will stand up to criticism.

The Inquiry Method for Restructuring Schemata

Observation and guided questioning can help pupils acquire new schemata.

Teacher's Statement	*Pupil's Response*
1. List what you observed. Tell me what you saw, tasted, heard, read.	Describes the observed phenomena.
2. What facts or events go together?	Groups the items.
3. What is the common thread among these items?	Gives common factors for grouping.
4. What do you call each of the groups?	Labels the groups.
5. Do the items belong to one group only?	Examines the grouping.
6. Let's try to find another way to group the items.	Considers alternative ways to group.
7. What is the common thread among the items in the new grouping?	Identifies a common factor for the new grouping.
8. In the light of these groupings, what concepts (labels, schemata) do we now have?	Summarizes by giving final grouping.

When the above outline is used, pupils' responses constitute the cognitive process that develops the schema. For instance, if you wanted to introduce a schema for democratic government, you might ask pupils to read about such governments as those of ancient Egypt and Mexico and those of modern Japan, France, and Britain. Once pupils have information, you may begin the questioning. Pupils should group the various governments (Step 2); examine the groups (Step 5); offer alternative grouping (Step 6); and give final labels (Step 8). When pupils perform these processes, they have a strong stake in the schema. *They* have manipulated the data by grouping and labeling the various features of governments and by defending their suggested groupings and final concept. Inasmuch as the concept and categories that are developed reflect a way of structuring the world, you must ask for and accept alternative ways for grouping the various governments and elicit suggestions according to a variety of vantage points.

Joseph Nussbaum and Shimshon Novick have proposed an instructional strategy for accommodating conceptual conflict.[8] The strategy consists of three phases: (1) exposing alternative frameworks, (2) creating conceptual conflict, and (3) encouraging cognitive accommodation. Nussbaum and Novick knew that many students have the misconception that matter is continuous. Students sometimes say, for instance, that between the particles in the air there are more particles (or bacteria, pollutants, oxygen, or the like) or simply "more air." In the teacher's view, it is desirable for students to replace this misconception about the nature of matter with the view that a gas is composed of tiny invisible particles and that there is an empty space (a vacuum) between the particles. To this end, Nussbaum and Novick designed an "exposing event"—the evacuation of air from a closed flask by use of a hand pump. This event forced each student to take a position with regard to the possible existence of "empty space" (a vacuum). The following is an account of what happened.[9]

Lesson 1—Exposing Alternative Frameworks and Creating Conceptual Conflict

Our lesson opens with the presentation of a flask containing air and an evacuating hand pump, whose operation is demonstrated. . . . Learning set is established when pupils feel the pump's sucking effect against their fingers (the laughter generated contributes to a relaxed atmosphere in the classroom).

[8] Joseph Nussbaum and Shimshon Novick, "Alternative Frameworks: Conceptual Conflict and Accommodation," *Instructional Science* 11 (1982): 183–200.
[9] Nussbaum and Novick, "Alternative Frameworks," pp. 190–96.

Phase 1: "Which part of the flask is left without air?" "Where do you place the 'empty space' (vacuum) in your model?"—setting an "exposing event."

> . . . We would need a much better evacuating pump to take out most of the air from this flask. Let's connect the flask to the pump and push the piston in and out about ten times. Let's assume we've removed half the air from the flask.
>
> Of course, we can't see the air in the flask. Let's pretend that each of us is given a pair of "magic magnifying spectacles" through which we can actually see air. I want each of you to imagine you're looking at the air in the flask through your "magic spectacles." What would you see? I am giving each of you a sheet of paper with two drawings of a flask in outline—one for the air before we used the pump and one for the air remaining after we removed half of it. Draw the air in the two flasks on the sheet, as it would look through the "magic spectacles," before and after the partial evacuation.

The teacher, moving around the classroom, selects representatives of each type of drawing. Each representative is sent to the blackboard to reproduce his/her speculated picture of the state of the air in the flask "before" and "after." Several flask outlines were prepared beforehand on the blackboard by the teacher. Soon we have three to seven different depictions of the air in the evacuated flask on the blackboard. The teacher writes each contributor's name above his/her drawing and adds a very short description of the drawing. At this point the blackboard looks like [Exhibit 4.2] without the "reasons" which are filled in later in the lesson.

A few procedural comments are in order here. In order to create an atmosphere of free debate, somewhat analogous to one which may exist among a group of scientists, we propose the following:

1. The teacher is advised to refrain from any hint of value judgment—all drawings are equally accepted. The teacher may say: "that's interesting"; "here's a new idea." He should not say: "good," "fine," etc.
2. Neat, accurate drawings and descriptions using chalk of different colors definitely help students to differentiate meaningfully between the alternative suggestions, thereby contributing to more active and meaningful class participation.
3. It is desirable that the teacher always refer to drawings by the contributor's name—"who wants to support David's drawing?"; "who thinks Benny's drawing isn't right?"; "According to Gideon's theory, the air wants to burst out"; "Sarah's theory doesn't show us from where the evacuated air is missing."
4. A class will not always offer as many as seven conceptions; more generally four or five alternatives will surface. While the teacher should try to encourage many suggestions, it is not necessary to labor the point. We have found that as few as three conceptions are sufficient as a start toward a very interesting discussion.

Exhibit 4.2   Blackboard Array of Students' Preconceptions

	1 David	2 Sarah	3 Ruth	4 Gideon	5 Miriam	6 Dan	7 Benny
Description	The air that is left is on the top; below it there is a vacuum	Air remains on the bottom; above it there is a vacuum	Air fills the flask, but there is less of it	The air remains near the side arm	Most of the air is on the bottom, then less and less on top— a vacuum	Air fills the flask, but there is less of it	The remaining air is in the middle and around it there is a vacuum
before evacuation after							after
Reasons	The air sinks because its specific gravity is greater than the vacuum	A gas flows, so the air flows to fill the flask	Air has nearly no weight; very light things rise	We pulled the air from this opening; the remaining air concentrates there and wants to push out	It's like what we learned about the atmosphere in our geography lessons	This is like the second drawing but it would look like this if a little dwarf could get in and see	I can't give a reason; I just feel it should be that way

Source: Joseph Nussbaum and Shimshon Novick, ''Alternative Frameworks: Conceptual Conflict and Accommodations,'' *Instructional Science* 11(1982): 192.

Phase 2. "Give reasons for your description"—deepening awareness of the component of each alternative preconception.

> . . . Now that we have all these interesting descriptions, I suggest we go back and ask each contributor just why he thinks the air looks like that after we took out half of it with the pump. Anyone else is also welcome to add reasons for the drawing that looks the best to him.

The reasons offered for the drawing are shown in [Exhibit 4.2], as they appeared on the blackboard array. During this phase, arguments develop in a lively give-and-take atmosphere—there is a heightening of intellectual and emotional tension. We tell the students, however, that we want to concentrate first on reasons supporting each hypothesis and delay counter-arguments for the next phase of the lesson—the open debate.

> Now that we clearly understand each of your drawings, we have a problem. We received quite different suggestions from you. Can we accept all of them? Is there one which is better than the others? Which one is the most reasonable? How shall we find out? Shall we take a poll? (Students explain why a democratic poll is not a scientific method.) It is true that a poll is not the right way to find out. Nevertheless, let's find out how you all feel about this—just to see "which way the wind is blowing."

By taking a poll, one gets of course a different distribution in each class, but we have noticed a pattern. In the sixth and seventh grade classes we have taught, drawings 1, 3, and 4 received the most support. What do they have in common? Well, they all picture the air as one big "chunk" which is found in some defined part of the flask, and where the air was removed (by the pump) a vacuum is left.

Another comment on classroom "atmosphere" is in order here. With this "poll of public opinion," pupils become more involved and very curious to find out who gave the "correct" description.

Phase 3: "Pros and cons"—debating the issue. Sharpening awareness of alternative preconceptions.

> Well, it seems you're all very eager to find out how the air should really look through our magic magnifying spectacles. We should look at the logic of each position and try to see how it fits with other experiments we could do with air. Now break up into groups and see what you can come up with to defend or refute each of the drawings.

In classes used to working in small groups, the argument is especially lively and sometimes heated. At this point, even the more reticent students become involved. Interestingly enough, no critical remarks (pro or con) were made about Dan's drawing (No. 6). Why? It would seem that at this stage, the idea that the air could be in "chunks," with empty spaces between them, is so foreign that no need is felt to argue against it.

At the conclusion of Phase 3, after students have had a chance to give considerable thought to the key question of where the vacuum exists in the evacuated flask, we judge that all the students in the class have become aware of their own conceptions by presenting them verbally and by confronting other conceptions of their peers. This confrontation, we believe, introduces the seeds of "conceptual conflict" or "cognitive dissonance" that will mainly build up later in the lessons. We are now ready for the next phase.

Phase 4: "What makes air compressible?"—preconceptions in conflict with a reexamined phenomenon—a "discrepant event."

Our first lesson ends with the demonstration of a phenomenon that will hopefully lead to an accommodation in students' cognitive structures—that is, get them to see the need for the existence of empty space inside any sample of air (or other gas).

> Let's leave our "hot debate" for a moment. I'd like you to recall what we found out about compressing gases, liquids and solids. Let's compress some air in this syringe . . . (demonstration) . . . You all remember that we couldn't compress a liquid or a solid like that. I wonder—does compressing a gas like this raise any questions for you . . . does it make you wonder . . . ?

Either on their own initiative or with some help from the teacher, students arrive at the following query: How can you force one half of the air, which is in the cylinder, into the remaining space which is already occupied by air?

> After all, we know from everyday experience with things that aren't gases that you can't take their place without moving them away (two pupils can't sit at the same time on the same seat). So how does the air in the bottom of the syringe allow more air to occupy the same space when we push down the plunger?

What in the nature and the structure of air makes it so compressible?

> We've come to the end of our lesson today. Shall we continue with this problem next time? (A chorus of assent.) OK. Then think about it until tomorrow. I suggest you try to see which of the drawings on the blackboard could help you to best explain how we can compress air in a syringe.

Lesson 2. Cognitive Dissonance Leads to Accommodation and the Invention of a New Model

Our second lesson begins with a review of the various descriptions of the air left in the flask, with the help of duplicated sheets showing the blackboard array of descriptions, drawings and reasons (see [Exhibit 4.2]).

Let's go back now to our discussion about air in a syringe, which I hope you've thought about since our last lesson. Here you see how I can easily make 100 cc of air occupy only 50 cc (teacher demonstrates). What questions can be asked about this peculiar phenomenon?

Students talk about this in small groups or in class discussions and the following three questions emerge on the blackboard: (1) How can two quantities of air in the syringe, each occupying 50 cc (together, 100 cc) occupy only 50 cc after the plunger is pushed in? (2) Why can this be done only with a gas, like air, and not with a liquid or a solid? (3) What is special about the structure of air that allows it to be compressed?

Now, as you remember, I asked you at the end of our last lesson to think about which of the seven descriptions of the air in the evacuated flask might help us to answer these questions.

Students begin to search for some relationship among the various speculated "structures," represented by the drawings, and the observation of a phenomenon unique to gases: their compressibility. The kinds of responses offered will of course vary from group to group. However, in every class that we have taught, at least one student suggests something to the effect that,

Maybe air is always like Dan's drawing (number 6)—even when we don't remove any of it. Maybe air is made of little pieces with empty space in between.

In one class a student suggested this model (basically not too different from a particle model):

Maybe air is like a sponge. Maybe the air is like the sponge material itself and between the chunks of air there is empty space like the holes in the sponge.

The discussion now becomes very lively; students are personally very involved in the debate. They try to show how their own drawings could explain the air's compressibility and to deal with the criticism of their classmates. Students are seen using paper and pencil and hand gestures to help their arguments for their picture of the air's structure and behavior in the flask and in the syringe. We have found that the suggestion that drawing 6 explains the air's compressibility is at first rejected by many students. For them the idea that there is a "vacuum" in ordinary air is just too strange. The teacher, while refraining from expressing preference for any one drawing, presses the "anti-particle" students to offer a better explanation of the air's compressibility. Most pupils begin to realize that despite the strangeness of the "particles in a vacuum" idea, it does explain both phenomena—the evacuation and the compression of air. More and more students join the "particle camp" and even volunteer to argue against their previous opinions. One argument against the particle idea should be noted. Some students said:

> If we assume there is empty space among particles, then why doesn't water rise into a glass of air inverted in a bowl of water?
>
> What holds the particles separated from each other if there is just empty space between them? Why don't the particles just fall down and pile up at the bottom of the flask?

The teacher acknowledges these questions and even writes them on the blackboard as good questions to be kept in mind. These responses show the need to introduce inherent motion of particles as part of the model, to explain pressure phenomena. This additional aspect is developed in subsequent lessons by again invoking "cognitive dissonance" and accommodation.

After the particle picture has become the focus of discussion and its supporters are increasing, the teacher intervenes to demonstrate the compression once again, but this time compressing 100 cc of air to just 20 cc.

> If we assume the air is really composed of particles what does this compression suggest about the amount of space taken up by the particles compared with the empty space between them?

Students suggest the empty space is much larger than the space taken up by the particles:

> If I had pressed much harder on the plunger, I could have compressed the air even more. But even if we used a steel syringe and exerted tremendous force, we still couldn't compress the air to zero volume. We always reach a minimum volume. Why?

Students suggest that the limit of compression is reached when there is no more empty space between the particles.

Our second lesson ends with the teacher's statement:

> Indeed the picture scientists have accepted is that of air composed of particles and empty space among them. The question which now arises is why the air resists being compressed. Why do we have to press on the plunger to keep the air compressed? We'll talk about this problem next time.

Communication Theory and the Restructuring of Schemata

Teaching is an act of communication. As such, it is governed by the same rules as other communicative acts. Certain norms exist for successful interaction between reader and author. These norms stress the importance of truth and a concern that the reader accept the ideas expressed. The normative ideal of communication contrasts with "strategic" forms of communication, such as propaganda, lying, misleading, deceiving, and manipulating, which are "parasitic" on writing aimed at creating sincere understanding.

The German philosopher Jürgen Habermas has summarized the elements essential to communication. Further, he has discussed procedures for resolving conflicts in communication procedures that apply in helping pupils restructure their existing schemata when confronted with what they perceive as untruthful or unacceptable ideas:[10]

1. The author should be comprehensible to the reader in the linguistic sense—the reader must follow the syntax.
2. The author must have knowledge to share. Whatever knowledge, observation, or interpretation is stated should be true. If pupils do not believe the statements, they should be instructed to compare the evidence and arguments of the author with the arguments of those who doubt. Pupils must feel free to call into question whatever has been written and to try to arrive at a decision regarding the truth or falsity of the statement by considering only the strength of the evidence and the arguments. Decisions should be based on a rational consensus of class members and not on the teacher's position or the popularity of pupils with particular views. Such rationality in the classroom may seem unrealistic, and its occurrence is probably most unusual; however, it is impossible to arrive at true communication without moving in this direction.
3. The author must be perceived as truthful, with no intention to deceive readers. If readers do not perceive truthfulness upon initial contact with a book, they should continue far enough in their reading of the text to see if the author shows the implications—truth—of what he or she is saying. The conventional practice of having pupils recognize bias in writing is relevant here. The presence of emotionally laden words, the omission of facts, and the use of overgeneralizations are grounds for doubting truthfulness.
4. In order to communicate, whatever the author says or recommends must be right and acceptable in terms of the reader's normative schemata. At times a teacher may have to help pupils see how the author's ideas are consistent with their norms and values and their social context. It may also be necessary to have a critical discussion of the pupils' norms. This point has much to do with restructuring of schemata. When differences in beliefs and values block communication, the reader has three options: stop reading the text, continue to read the text and feign agreement with the points made in order to please the teacher (a strategic form of communication), or enter into a discussion for the purpose of arriving at a rational agreement.

[10] Thomas McCarthy, *The Critical Theory of Jürgen Habermas* (Cambridge, Mass.: MIT Press, 1981).

**Activity 4.2   Reading for a Different Purpose—Perceived
Truthfulness**

Select any narrative you use in your classroom. Ask pupils first to read the
story for *what* the author says. Then ask them to reread the story for the
purpose of deciding *how* and *why* the author said it. Was the author truthful?

Help the pupils reread by asking them to provide instances of the author's logical and emotional arguments, facts, and allegations. Ask them to
identify the author's values with respect to honesty, friends, nature, money,
and so on. Does he or she make fun of persons and manners?

Ask these kinds of questions: What does this character do that is connected with the author's values? How does the author tell what honesty or
some other value means to him or her? Why does the author think the value
is important? What reasons does the character give for valuing *X*? Is the
author ashamed or proud about the value *X*? Why do you think the author
has this value? Do your perceive the author as truthful? Why? Why not?

Teachers who organize a critical discussion when pupils are unable to
accept the writer's point of view may try to restructure schemata in
several ways. First, they may try to see what is present in the pupils'
situations that makes the author's ideas appropriate. Perhaps the author is
saying something that is really consistent with the readers' norms. If there
is no connection, then teachers must take a look at the readers' norms.
What are the consequences of the beliefs held by the readers? To what
extent do these beliefs contribute or fail to contribute to the concerns of
human life, to generally accepted needs and wants (physical and mental
well-being, self-respect, self-actualization, control over aspects of one's
life)? Critical discussion will work only if the participants know and say
what they really want.

Why is it important to engage in critical discussion of those ideas in
text that appear to be unacceptable? Because the author may offer a
better response to some of the readers' central concerns than their existing schemata. Comprehending text means making sense of it by relating it
to one's own situation and seeing how it contributes to the needs of
human life.

Children come to school with the symbolic universe of the family—
as Rodriguez says, the language of intimacy. Increasingly, the school will
introduce content that challenges the norms of the home and the local
community. In making the transition, children must examine norms in
light of new ideas about the human situation.

Unlike the preschool child, beginning readers have the ability to
distinguish between fantasy and perception, between impulse and obliga-
tion. They can learn to look at reading selections from the perspectives of
others representing the familiar roles of family and community members.

Activity 4.3   Reading from Different Perspectives

A device for restructuring schemata is the repeated reading of text from different perspectives. The requirements are (a) a text that is relevant to the schemata to be restructured and that allows for alternative interpretations; (b) the assignment of pupils to various viewpoints; (c) a discussion by the readers; and (d) a switching of points of view.

Select one story, article, or book. Have pupils first read it to get the gist of the material. Then do the following:

1. Decide upon the perspectives that would give rise to important dimensions of the topic or theme. Young children may use the frameworks of those with different social roles—father, mother, sister, doctor, driver. Mature readers may use theoretical frameworks with which they are familiar—a Marxist or a Freudian perspective, for example. You may want to demonstrate the way in which a person with a given perspective would respond to a class of situations.
2. Have pupils briefly state the perspective they will use. The statement should include major concerns, arguments, and values associated with the perspective. Assumptions underlying the viewpoint may be given by mature readers.
3. Have pupils identify the essential features of the selection from the perspective chosen.
4. Have pupils, using the perspectives, tell how the selection is different from or similar to other familiar selections.
5. Have pupils decide if there are elements missing in the selection that would be important to the perspective.
6. Have pupils tell why the missing elements are important to the perspective.
7. Have pupils give their judgment of the selection.
8. Repeat the steps but from another perspective. (This activity may occur at a subsequent time.)
9. Have pupils make an overall conclusion about the selection after considering the points raised from the perspectives taken.

In assessing the value of this activity, note changes in pupils' schemata as indicated by their conclusions and points of view about the selection analyzed.

They can learn that different persons see the same situation from different perspectives, with different intentions, wants, feelings, and meanings.

Pupils in late childhood can apply an even wider range of perspectives. They are ready to consider how those with different perspectives are responding to human needs. As adolescents, most readers are capable of reading from a number of perspectives based on various theories and views about religion, politics, education, economics, art, psychology, medicine, and the like. Adolescents are able to treat their own views and the author's as hypothetical—to separate themselves from inherited

Activity 4.4   Identifying Conflicting Preconceptions

Pupils sometimes find it difficult to accept ideas in their reading because of conflicting preconceptions of a moral, cultural, or physical nature.

Take a selection—complete text, chapter, or article—that you intend to use in your classroom. Identify the major assumptions underlying the author's conclusions or main ideas. Before asking pupils to read the selection, present the assumptions and ask pupils whether they agree with them or not, giving their reasons. These responses will reveal ideas that need restructuring if the reader is to accept the information given. The following categories and examples illustrate typical assumptions underlying various materials.

Moral Assumptions (social studies, literature)

Relativism: There are different points of view. Things are not black or white, right or wrong. Rules are made by people and can be modified to fit circumstances. Behavior should be judged in terms of motive and consequences.
Authority: There are those who have authority over our behavior (legal authority). This authority should restrain our actions. On the other hand, there are equals (peers and friends) with whom we cooperate because we identify with them. Sometimes the values of the peer society conflict with those of persons in positions of authority.

Cultural Assumptions (social studies, literature)

Children's role: Children should participate with adults in the serious concerns going on about them. Pupils should be able to effect change and set standards for themselves.
Social class: There is a rank-order among people striving for social recognition—upper class, middle class, and lower class. People in different classes hold different values. Social class affects children's motives, actions, and long-term development.
Conflict: The presence of multicultural patterns in our society accounts for confusion about acceptable standards.
Historical time: The Peruvian Indians had extensive systems of religion, farming, and industry nearly 5,000 years ago that lasted until Pizarro arrived in 1532. Using the analogy of a clock, we can say that Peruvian Indian culture shows twenty-four hours while United States history from the time of George Washington to now shows less than an hour.

Physical Assumptions (science, social studies)

Nature: We should not see nature as our enemy—something to be feared and destroyed. Neither should we worship nature. We should strive to understand nature and the human conditions within it.
Cause: Most explanations of physical phenomena are based upon reason and logic rather than upon direct observation of forces within the phenomena.
Variability: The attempt to make persons uniform—biologically, emotionally, or intellectually—is a betrayal of the evolutionary thrust that has put human beings at the apex.

Uncertainty: All knowledge is limited—everything is at best a guess. (Granted there is a high probability that the chair you are sitting on is indeed a chair, even though it might be changed in some way from yesterday or last year.)

---

roles, norms, and values. They are at an appropriate stage to engage in critical discussion. They are open to the beliefs of others and can weigh evidence in support of new ideas and the inherited norms with which they appear to conflict.

SUMMARY

The influence of students' preconceptions and misconceptions upon their reading of texts has been underestimated. Readers often do not really change their ideas as a consequence of their reading. It takes energy to unlearn a misconception. Just giving the student an explanation for how and why something is true is not enough. The student must actively create meaning from that explanation. Teachers need to find out the views that pupils bring with them to reading lessons. Critical misconceptions must be restructured. Classroom practices that facilitate the restructuring of readers' ideas generally call for: (a) creating a situation that requires the students to invoke their preconceptions; (b) encouraging students to state their preconceptions clearly, thereby becoming aware of the elements in the preconceptions; (c) encouraging confrontation, bringing out in discussion the difference between the student's view and those of others; (d) creating a conflict between exposed preconceptions and some situation that the preconceptions cannot explain; and (e) supporting the student's search for resolution and accommodation.

Useful Reading

Anderson, R. C., R. J. Spiro, and W. E. Montague, eds. *Schooling and the Acquisition of Knowledge*. Hillsdale, N.J.: Erlbaum, 1977.

Applebee, A. N. "Children's Construct of Stories and Related Genres as Measured with Repertory Grid Techniques." *Research in the Teaching of English* 10 (1976): 226–38

Cole, M., and S. Scribner. "Cross-Cultural Studies of Memory and Cognition." In *Perspective on the Development of Memory and Cognition*, eds. R. V. Kail, Jr., and J. W. Hagen. Hillsdale, N.J.: Erlbaum, 1977.

di Sibio, Mary. "Memory for Connected Discourse: A Constructivist View." *Review of Educational Research* 52 (1982): 149–74.

Hyman, R. A. *Strategic Questioning*. Englewood Cliffs, N.J.: Prentice-Hall, 1980.

Kuhn, T. S. *The Structure of Scientific Revolutions*. Chicago: University of Chicago Press, 1970.

Riegel, K. F. "Dialectic Operations: The Final Period of Cognitive Development." *Human Development* 16 (1973): 346–70.

5 Metacognition in Reading Comprehension

SELF-KNOWLEDGE

TASK KNOWLEDGE
  The Strategy of Self-Instruction
  A Question-Recognition Strategy
  Reading to Remember

SELF-MONITORING

SUMMARY

Overview

Thus far three goals for effective comprehension have been identified: knowledge of the concepts treated in the passage (relevant schemata and their activation) so that elaboration can be made, spontaneous generation of inferences and predictions based upon the implicit information in the text, and elaboration of important aspects of the text rather than ideas of lesser consequence.

Although teachers have had considerable success in helping pupils under their direction to use personal experiences in the process of inferring while reading, they have been less successful in getting pupils to spontaneously apply such strategies to fresh materials. Conscious control of effective strategies independent of the teacher is not always realized.

One of this chapter's central purposes is to look at promising approaches to the difficult task of teaching pupils both to be aware of the reading strategies they are using and to monitor their own reading. These approaches relate to *metacognition*. The original Greek prefix *meta* gave a transcendent character to whatever it qualified. In our times, newly coined words beginning with *meta* reflect a view of things from the outside, a more abstract level, and a mature understanding. In reading, metacognition transcends cognition by enabling individuals not just to use particular strategies, but to be aware of the importance of these strategies and how to appraise them. Metacognition emphasizes broad control processes rather than highly specific task strategies. It addresses the problems of pupils who have been taught appropriate strategies for comprehending but fail to employ them. Metacognitive processes in reading are:

a. *Self-knowledge*—recognizing one's strengths and weaknesses in comprehending. The child's view of self as a reader is an instance.
b. *Task knowledge*—knowing the importance of matching a comprehension task with an appropriate reading or memory strategy. Appreciation of having a perceived purpose for reading, a plan for action, and ways to assess progress and to revise are important parts of task knowledge.
c. *Self-monitoring*—being aware whether one has or has not understood the text and knowing the value of what to do when failing to comprehend. The so-called "debugging" practices of backtracking and reading ahead when incomprehensible text is encountered are examples of self-monitoring.

SELF-KNOWLEDGE

Learners have perceptions and feelings about themselves as readers that affect their performance. "Learned helplessness"—the perceived inability to overcome failure—is particularly self-defeating. After "helpless" children experience failure, they tend to attribute their failure to lack of ability. In contrast, successful readers deal with failure in other ways—self-monitoring, self-instruction, and reanalysis of the task at hand.[1]

Knowing that learning-disabled children lack context sensitivity, Pflaum and Pascarella developed a program to teach such children, ages eight to twelve, how to use context information as a means of raising their level of comprehension. The program had two parts. One set of twelve lessons featured error detection. Pupils learned to identify oral errors that another person made on tape and then to identify their own. (An example of a serious error would be one that caused the meaning to be altered— *back parent* for *back porch*.) Children determined the seriousness of an error first by judging errors made by others while reading and then by judging their own.

The second set of twelve lessons focused on integrating knowledge of meaning from context with phonic cues to identify words and make self-corrections. The results were an increase in the use of context clues, especially for those who read at second-grade level or better.

---

[1] C. S. Dweck and B. G. Licht, "Learned Helplessness and Intellectual Achievement," in *Human Helplessness: Theory and Applications,* ed. J. Garber and M. E. P. Seligman (New York: Academic Press, 1980).

Inasmuch as the program encouraged pupils to decide whether errors were serious and self-corrections accurate, we might wonder if such a program would have a different effect on children who do not have a sense of control over their learning. Would pupils who attribute success to external forces, who see no connection between their efforts and success, be helped or confused when given control in deciding about errors?

Pascarella and Pflaum wondered about this question.[2] They tried to find out whether differences in orientation regarding the sources of success and failure would interact with the strategy. The original program was revised to provide a version in which the teacher determined errors as well as a version in which the pupil determined errors. The results were that children who were internally oriented achieved more with the pupil-determined procedure; externally oriented pupils had higher scores when the teacher determined errors. However, the results of this study provoke more questions. Can externally oriented children be helped to acquire an internal sense of control, which would have long-term learning benefits? Was the training program long enough to effect a change in pupils' attributions?

I know of no simple solution to the problem of learned helplessness. There are exhortations about the importance of having teachers and pupils expect success. In addition, the literature on self-worth and school learning offers general principles. Some of the most interesting literature in this area is that by Martin Covington and Richard Berry, Richard de Charms, and Bernard Weiner.[3]

Covington and Berry stress the importance of pupils' being free to make errors, to reveal (temporary) ignorance, and to risk trying their hardest. They recommend that pupils learn to organize their own learning by dividing tasks into manageable subparts, making hard tasks easy by pinpointing the sources of difficulty, and setting performance goals in light of their own purposes.

De Charms and Weiner also point to the positive consequences from giving pupils control over their own learning. De Charms refers to pupils who are *origins*—in personal control of events—in contrast with those who are *pawns*—helpless in the hands of others. A person becomes an origin partly because of skillful goal setting, planning, and acceptance of responsibility for actions. Weiner has drawn attention to *locus of control*—whether a person sees achievement as caused by external forces,

[2] E. T. Pascarella and S. W. Pflaum, "The Interaction of Children's Attributions and Level of Control over Error Correction in Reading Instruction," *Journal of Educational Psychology* (1981): 77–81.

[3] Martin V. Covington and Richard C. Berry, *Self-Worth and School Learning* (New York: Holt, Rinehart and Winston, 1976); Richard de Charms, *Enhancing Motivation: A Change in the Classroom* (New York: Irvington Publishers, 1976); Bernard Weiner, "A Theory of Motivation for Some Classroom Experiences," *Journal of Educational Psychology* 71 (1971): 3–25.

such as task difficulty and luck, or by forces within, such as ability and effort. Successful pupils do not view failure as a threat, for it does not necessarily reflect on their ability and can be set right by effort.

Initiation of questions and other behavior associated with the active reader as presented in Chapter 2 are steps toward helping pupils become success-oriented, origins rather than pawns. In addition, it is important to let pupils know the value of asking their own questions and of understanding the rationale for particular learning strategies, not just carrying them out.

The child's schema for reading bears on locus of control. Children who perceive the importance of actively seeking and creating meaning from text before, during, and after reading are more likely to enjoy reading than are pupils who see themselves controlled by the text.

Evidence that fifth- and sixth-graders can improve in their recognition that success is under their own control through the skillful use of their own efforts is found in the Productive Thinking Program.[4]

This program consists of instructional material in which each lesson introduces a complex problem drawn from a range of subject matters. The pupil is asked to read a selection and attempt to solve a problem it poses. The problems are accompanied by problem-solving strategies for the pupil to apply—discovering and formulating problems, organizing incoming information, generating ideas, asking effective questions, and reformulating problems in new ways. A story line is maintained through a narrative involving two schoolchildren. These story characters are models for the reader. The reader generates his or her own questions and ideas, then the models respond with theirs. The models are not perfect—they make mistakes, but they also profit from them. Children using the productive thinking lessons acquire a sense of their own ability to think and gain confidence in their ideas. They solve increasingly difficult problems (which require hard work), thereby strengthening the link between effort and outcome and reinforcing an image of self as the cause of success.

Exhibit 5.1, a sample page from the Productive Thinking Program, illustrates one of the strategies featured.

TASK KNOWLEDGE

Task knowledge as an aspect of metacognition is more than knowing a comprehension strategy—it is understanding the significance of the strategy. The assumption is that if the pupil can connect the use of the strategy to particular results, he or she will use it in the absence of a teacher. The practice of asking pupils to state what they are doing and why when

---

[4] Martin V. Covington, Lillian Davies, Richard S. Crutchfield, and Robert M. Ofton, Jr., *The Productive Thinking Program* (Columbus, Ohio: Charles Merrill, 1972).

Exhibit 5.1   The Productive Thinking Program: Basic Lesson 13, "The Puzzle of the Deep-Sea Dive"

> That's right. We've got to untangle things so that we can be clear about exactly *what* happened.

> And remember what Uncle John said about problems in which people are doing things? We also have to figure out *who* and *why*, as well as *what*.

> We'll have to think about what each person's thoughts and feelings were, and the reasons he had for doing what he did.

Jim and Lila are taking a good first step by reflecting a while on the problem before plunging into it.

Did you do this, too, when you worked on the problem by yourself? If not, here is another chance to reflect a bit—to decide just what the *questions* are before you try to come up with *answers*.

Source: Martin V. Covington, Lillian Davies, Richard S. Crutchfield, and Robert M. Ofton, Jr., The Productive Thinking Program (Columbus, Ohio: Charles Merrill, 1972).

learning a strategy is one way to help them make the connection. For example, the following dialogue sometimes occurs in teaching a strategy for making inferences:

T: "What is it that we have been doing before we read each story?"

S: "We talk about our lives and our experiences with some of the ideas that are in the story and we predict what will happen in the story."

T: "Why do we compare our experiences with the ideas given in the story?"

S: "The comparison will help us understand the story."

The use of modeling, as in the productive thinking lessons, is another way to connect the use of a strategy with its consequences. The probability of pupils' applying a strategy on their own is increased if the teacher has had them generalize for themselves the strategy employed by the model and the results that followed. Of course, pupils need opportunities to see how well they are implementing the strategy and to find out for themselves the benefits that follow.

Task knowledge also means having broad controlling strategies. Three such strategies are self-instruction, question recognition, and reading to remember.

The Strategy of Self-Instruction

Essentially, self-instruction (self-interrogation, verbal monitoring, or thinking aloud) aims at helping learners be aware of their own cognitive processes. Accordingly, pupils learn to ask themselves questions: "Why am I doing this?" "What am I to do?" "How shall I do it?" "Did I succeed?"

A pupil who has acquired the self-instruction strategy might approach a specific reading task—say, finding a topic sentence—by asking and answering questions:

- "What is it I have to do?" (problem definition)
- "I have to find the topic sentence of the paragraph." (focusing attention)
- "The topic sentence is what the paragraph is about. I start by looking for a sentence that sums up the details or tells what the paragraph is about." (plan of action)
- "I haven't found it." (evaluation)
- "That's all right." (self-encouragement)
- "The topic sentence might be a definition or a combination of a question and answer." (revision)
- "I'll try my new plan." (coping)

Another example of a self-instructional learning strategy for comprehension: "I've learned three things. First, I ask myself what the main idea of the story is—what the story is about. Second, I learn important details of the story as I go along. The order of the main events and their sequence are important details. Third, I ask myself how the characters feel and why."

In teaching self-instructional strategies, the teacher first models, talking aloud to the class, while attacking a reading task. Next, the pupils overtly rehearse the strategy shown by the teacher by telling what they are doing while they do it—defining the task, stating what they have to do, focusing their attention, stating their plan of action, revising the plan when the original plan doesn't work, giving themselves verbal reassurance ("I goofed but that's OK"), revising, and trying again.

The overt rehearsals are followed by covert rehearsals. Here, pupils attack the reading task, but this time they *think* to themselves the questions. Finally, pupils practice using the strategy in approaching reading tasks in a variety of other materials. The same procedure—modeling, overt rehearsal, covert rehearsal, practice with other material—is carried out with a number of comprehension tasks, such as finding supporting evidence for a generalization, locating specific information, inferring tone or mood, and drawing conclusions. In every case, the elements of problem definition, focus, plan of action, evaluation, and coping, if necessary, should be present.

A Question-Recognition Strategy

Some years ago Edgar Dale wrote of three levels of reading comprehension: (a) *reading the lines,* by which pupils obtain information explicitly stated; (b) *reading between the lines,* by which pupils discover implicit meanings of text; and (c) *reading beyond the lines,* whereby pupils interpret text in terms of their own personal values.[5] However, before pupils can engage in reading at these levels, they must know the difference between questions that are directly answerable from text (explicitly stated in text); questions whose answers can be logically inferred from the sentences in the passage (implicitly stated in the text); and questions that can only be answered if the reader's own background of experience suggests the answers (implicit in schema or script).

David Pearson and Dale Johnson have proposed a taxonomy for categorizing questions on the basis of their function and the source of likely answers.[6] I believe this taxonomy suggests an important way for helping pupils acquire the metacognitive knowledge whether questions are answerable and, if they are answerable, how.

The taxonomy features three categories—*text explicit, text implicit,* and *script (schemata) implicit.* Any *who, what, where, how, when* questions can fit any category, depending upon the text. For example, *why* usually calls for an answer regarding purpose. Purposes, however, may be directly stated, inferred from the sentences, or inferred from the reader's experiences. *What* frequently demands a fact for an answer. Yet, in

---

[5] Edgar Dale, "The Art of Reading," *The Newsletter* 32 (December 1966): 1–4.
[6] P. David Pearson and Dale D. Johnson, *Teaching Reading Comprehension* (New York: Holt, Rinehart and Winston, 1978); pp. 157–64.

some contexts, the answer may be stated; and in other contexts, the factual answer can only come from application of personal knowledge.

You may wish to see if you can categorize questions according to the Pearson and Johnson taxonomy. Read the following paragraph and then classify the four accompanying questions as text implicit, text explicit, or schemata implicit. Then compare your answers with those given.

> First were paraded the Indians, painted to their savage fashion, and decorated with tropical feathers, and with their national ornaments of gold. After these were borne various kinds of live parrots, together with stuffed birds and rare plants. Great care was taken to make a conspicuous display of Indian bracelets and other decorations of gold, which might give an idea of the wealth of the newly discovered region. After these, followed Columbus on horseback, surrounded by a brilliant cavalcade of Spanish chivalry.

What is the newly discovered region?
Why were the bracelets displayed?
How did the writer regard the Indians?
Where does the event take place?

The answer to the first question requires background information—a schema for the discovery of a New World by Columbus (script implicit). The second question requires a text explicit answer—to show the wealth of the new region. The answer to the third question is implicit in the text, as indicated by the writer's use of such words as *savage* (wild, uncivilized, animal). The fourth question can be answered by associating the desire to impress with the presence of Spanish chivalry; the answer—Spain—is text implicit.

A program for teaching young children question-answer relationships as a strategy for facilitating correct responses to questions has been developed and implemented by Raphael and Wonnacott.[7] This four-day intensive program introduced pupils to the concept of how questions are related to answers. Questions and corresponding answers from several different texts at each level of the question-answer taxonomy were illustrated. Pupils learned to explain how each category of questions (explicit, implicit, script) applied and how the response information was located. Gradually, pupils provided responses to questions independently.

All materials were based on familiar topics so as to maximize the possibility of success. Implementation of the program resulted in higher performance on a comprehension test and gave evidence that the question-recognition strategy transferred to reading improvement in the content fields.

[7] T. E. Raphael and C. A. Wonnacott, "Metacognitive Training in Question Answering Strategies Implemented in a 4th Grade Developmental Reading Program" (Paper presented at the National Reading Conference, Dallas, Texas, December 1981).

Exhibit 5.2   Three Kinds of Questions

Type 1

Where is the answer found?

Right There

The answer is in the story, easy to find. The words used to make the questions and the words that make the answer are Right There, in the same sentence.

Type 2

Think and Search

The answer is in the story, but a little harder to find. You would never find the words in the question and words in the answer in the same sentence, but would have to Think and Search for the answer.

Type 3

On My Own

The answer won't be told by words in the story. You must find the answer in your head. Think: "I have to answer this question On My Own, the story won't be much help."

Source: Taffy E. Raphael, "Question-Answering Strategies for Children," *Reading Teacher* 36 (November 1982):188.

Taffy Raphael refers to question-answer relationships as QARs.[8] As shown in Exhibit 5.2, in Raphael's program, *Right There* refers to text explicit questions, *Think and Search* refers to text implicit questions, and *On My Own* refers to schema implicit questions. Little divergence is expected in answers to *Right There* QARs. However, more divergence occurs as pupils deal with *Think and Search* and *On My Own* QARs. In learning QARs, the readers should progress from shorter to longer texts, from group to independent activities, and from the easier task of recognizing an answer to the more difficult task of creating a response from more than one source of information. The following is an outline of the four lessons used in training pupils to find where the answers to questions lie.

- *Lesson One:* The first lesson includes four phases: In the first phase, pupils are given a passage plus questions whose answers and QARs have already been identified. Pupils discuss why the questions and answers represent particular QARs. In the second phase, pupils are

[8] Taffy E. Raphael, "Question-Answering Strategies for Children," *Reading Teacher* 36 (November 1982): 186–90.

given passages, questions, and responses; but this time they identify the QAR for each. In the third phase, pupils are given other passages and questions and are required to read the passage, decide on the appropriate QAR, and supply the answer to the question.

- *Lesson Two:* Longer passages (75 to 150 words) with up to five questions per passage are used. Pupils may work through the first passage as a group and then continue independently.
- *Lesson Three:* Passages about the length of a basal reading story are used. A passage is divided into approximately four sections and is followed by six questions, each from a different category.
- *Lesson Four:* Material found in the classroom is used—basal story or social studies or science chapter. Pupils respond to a long passage (600 to 800 words) accompanied by six questions for each QAR category. Pupils read the passage, respond to each question by identifying the QAR, and then give the answer.

Reading to Remember

Any appropriate strategy for remembering rests on identifying main points. These main points may be saved in some form—outline, notes, summary. The points should be mentally rehearsed and the text skimmed at a later time. You and I know that persons are less likely to remember ideas that are of less personal interest and those that counter preexisting beliefs. But pupils may have to be made aware of these facts so that they can give such ideas additional attention.

Knowledge of mnemonics is useful in recalling parts of a text. Examples are: saying the item to be remembered over and over, elaborating upon the item (making up a meaningful context in which to remember it), and categorizing the information.

Young children tend to overestimate what they will be able to remember. Therefore, one function of metacognitive instruction is to help the child to be informed about his or her capacity to remember and to see how the application of a plan for remembering increases what is recalled.

A generalizable study procedure in most plans is to read until one thinks he or she is ready for testing and then to self-test. Obviously, the child should recognize that the self-testing must match whatever is important to remember.

SELF-MONITORING

Being aware that one has not understood and knowing what to do about it are metacognitive matters. Self-checking and correcting are associated with good reading. Researchers have attempted to assess pupils' awareness that they have not understood by deliberately creating errors in the text—disorganizing passages, adding inappropriate transition words and inconsistent sentences—and then observing whether or not pupils noted the errors. For example, one group of investigators manipulated the content of simple stories.[9] One version contained logical information—*The hungry boy ate a hamburger.* The other version related deliberately arbitrary information—*The hungry boy took a nap.* Successful readers noted that the stories with arbitrary content were more difficult to learn and regulated their study time accordingly. Less successful readers did not. In fact, the less successful readers appeared less aware that arbitrary information is harder to learn and did not spontaneously monitor their reading comprehension. Schema theory helps in our explanation for the failure. Readers must have a schema that predisposes them to make sure that text makes sense. Further, they must have the relevant schema for whatever they are reading so that they form expectations about the text. Failure to confirm expectations signals a comprehension failure.

Sometimes pupils may not report inconsistencies and anomalies in text because they assume the writer made a mistake that can be ignored (children can be very generous); or they may draw on prior knowledge to supplement the information incorrectly presented. Perhaps too they have been taught not to question the text.

Evaluating one's own comprehension requires a concern for both standards and the process of comprehending. The degree to which one wants to comprehend depends upon one's purpose for reading. If a person is interested only in filling in some detail—such as a figure or location—the standard for comprehending may be low. On the other hand, to assimilate a point of view, a new procedure, or a concept requires a high standard.

Monitoring of comprehension gets better when pupils have personal reasons for reading the material and when they improve at processing text—at noting whether their reading is confirming their predictions. Self-questioning also helps by clarifying the relevance of what is read. Unless pupils try to connect the meanings of sentences, they are not likely to detect contradictions and inconsistencies in text. Hence, attempts are made to improve self-evaluation of comprehension by teaching the constructive processes underlying it.

Carol Capelli and Ellen Markham taught third- and sixth-graders to detect inconsistencies by having them read short stories, one sentence at a time, and answer a set of questions after each sentence.[10]

---

[9] R. Owings et al., "Spontaneous Monitoring and Regulation of Learning—A Comparison of Successful and Less Successful Fifth Graders," *Journal of Educational Psychology* 72 (1980): 250–56.

[10] C. A. Capelli and E. M. Markham, *Improving Comprehension Monitoring Through Training in Hypothesis Testing* (Palo Alto, Calif.: Stanford University Press, 1981).

The children were asked to make hypotheses about who the characters were, what was going on, why the characters did what they did, and where the story took place. Initially, the teacher modeled answers to the questions. Next, the children themselves answered the questions. The explicitness of the questions was gradually diminished until the children were simply describing their interpretations, while keeping the questions in mind. Later, the children read stories with inconsistencies and reported the problems they detected. They were to keep the questions in mind and "to think about everything that's going on in the story" as they read it.

Once readers recognize that they do not understand—that their purposes are not being met—what should they do? Common strategies for dealing with such difficulty are rereading, continuing reading, and seeking clarification in subsequent sections of the text. Skilled readers know when to keep reading and when to jump back and reread. These readers carry a set of questions, and, if the text suggests that these questions will be answered, they continue to read. If too many questions collect, they jump back to the sentences that led to the questions. These sentences they then reread to form a hypothesis that will allow them to cut down the number of unanswered questions. The hypothesis may be quite specific: Is it that a word is not understood? Is the sentence not understood? Or does the difficulty lie in the relationships among sentences?

Skilled readers who encounter text inconsistencies also spend more time on portions of the material containing the inconsistency, looking back at inconsistent material and at material immediately preceding the inconsistency.[11]

[11] A. Baker and R. Anderson, *Effects of Inconsistent Information on Text Processing,* Technical report no. 2031 (Urbana: Center for the Study of Reading, University of Illinois, May 1981).

Activity 5.1   Self-Instruction and Monitoring

Activity 5.1 capitalizes on the principle of cooperative peer teaching. Ask each pupil to select a reading comprehension task that he or she can do—finding the meaning of an unfamiliar word from context, finding a topic sentence, determining the sequence of events, identifying pronoun antecedents, interpreting metaphors and other figurative language, identifying speakers in dialogue, recognizing emotionally laden words, and others.

Once the task has been selected, ask the pupil to write an answer to each of the following questions about the task.

1.   What is it I have to do? Student defines problem and identifies focus of attention—for example, the problem may require determining the sequence of events.

Activity 5.1   *(Continued)*

---

2. How do I do it? Student forms plan of action. For example, he or she may decide to go about determining the sequence of events by looking for words indicating sequence (*first, next, last*), by imagining the events enfolding, or by anticipating the structure of the story—setting, events, character reaction, character's actions, consequences of the actions.

Children should be asked to answer Question 2 by writing what they would say to themselves while trying to solve their chosen tasks. The statement of task and plan of action should be reviewed. Class discussion of the plan may lead to additional ideas for accomplishing the task. The pupil who contributed the strategy should demonstrate its application, talking aloud as he or she attempts the task using an appropriate classroom text. (An appropriate selection offers opportunity to apply the strategy. If the task calls for identifying sequence of events, there must be a sequence of events in the selection.)

After the tasks have been defined and the strategies reviewed and demonstrated, pupils exchange tasks and accompanying strategies. Opportunity to first overtly and covertly practice the exchanged strategies may take place on subsequent days.

Activity 5.2   Recognizing the Sources of Answers to Questions

---

Using the text and questions below (or a text of your own choosing), have pupils tell whether the answer to each question is directly stated in the text (text explicit), inferred from the relationships among several sentences (text implicit), or generated primarily from the reader's own background (script implicit).

An animal and a plant are both living things. How can you tell which is which? Do both move? Yes, a daisy folds its petals together at night, and the sunflower moves its head from one side to the other as the sun goes across the sky. How then can you say that a cat is an animal but that the daisy and sunflower are not?

We know that the cat is an animal because it can't make its own food. The green plant can make its own food. An animal like a cat (or a human being, for that matter) can't.

The cat eats all sorts of things—fish, milk, mice, and birds. But that food is already "made." The cat can't join water, gas, and salts together to make the fish and milk. But green plants can make foods, just as complex as these, from the air and from what comes by its roots with the water from the soil.

1. How do we know that a cat is an animal? (answer is text explicit)
2. Why can't animals make their own food? (answer is script implicit)
3. Why do animals have to move about in order to find food while plants can feed best by staying in one place? (answer is text implicit)

SUMMARY

Metacognition is the conscious control of one's thinking about self, task, and the monitoring of performance. The problem of metacognition is to make readers aware of the difference between what they know and what they don't. In reading, metacognition means being aware of what one's purposes for reading are, how to proceed in achieving these purposes, and how to regulate progress through self-checking of comprehension and self-testing.

In this chapter, one aspect of self-knowledge—learned helplessness—is addressed. Productive thinking lessons are offered as an instructional answer to this problem.

Task knowledge is treated in this chapter as something more than knowing a comprehension strategy; it involves understanding the significance of the strategy—why it works. Techniques for helping readers acquire task knowledge, such as modeling a strategy for making inferences and helping readers form a self-interrogation strategy, are featured. Considerable attention is given to helping readers learn to recognize where the answers to questions can be found—to be conscious of when answers are text explicit, text implicit, or script implicit. Strategies for remembering—using mnemonics, saving main points, and being knowledgeable about one's own capacity to remember—are also considered.

The problem of monitoring and evaluating one's comprehension is examined in some detail, including ways to help readers independently be aware of when they do not understand text inconsistencies. Suggestions are given for helping readers develop awareness of self-questioning procedures and strategies for dealing with difficulties in comprehending text.

Useful Reading

Baker, L., and A. C. Brown. "Metacognition and the Reading Process." In *A Handbook of Reading Research,* ed. P. D. Pearson. New York: Plenum Press, 1983.

Flavell, J. H. "Metacognition and Cognitive Monitoring: A New Area of Cognitive-Developmental Enquiry." *American Psychologist* 34 (1979): 906–11.

Markham, E. M. "Comprehension Monitoring." In *Children's Oral Communication Skills.* New York: Academic Press, 1981.

Wong, Bernice, ed. "Metacognition and Learning Disabilities." *Topics in Learning and Learning Disabilities,* special issue (April 1982): 1–106.

6 Teaching Vocabulary from an Interactive View of Reading Comprehension

KINDS OF WORD MEANING

ASSUMPTIONS ABOUT LEARNING WORDS

TEACHING VOCABULARY AS A NETWORK OF IDEAS

SEMANTIC MAPPING

SEMANTIC FEATURE ANALYSIS

FRAYER MODEL

CONTEXTUAL PROCESSING

SUMMARY

Overview

The strong relationship between vocabulary knowledge and reading comprehension has long been known. What isn't known is why word knowledge is such a powerful factor in comprehension. Three hypotheses have been proposed: The *aptitude hypothesis* states that persons who score high on a test of vocabulary do so because of their mental agility, and this same thinking ability is what enables them to comprehend text so well. The instructional implication of this hypothesis is that, since vocabulary training won't affect mental ability, the difference in comprehension between high- and low-aptitude readers will remain the same in spite of such training.

The *instrumental hypothesis* claims that knowledge of individual word meaning is the primary factor responsible for reading comprehension. The instructional implication is that teaching vocabulary will improve reading comprehension. The more word meanings known, the better the comprehension.

The *knowledge hypothesis* holds that a person who knows a word well knows other words and ideas related to it. It is this network of ideas that enhances comprehension. When a person reads a particular word in text, it activates word associations and allows the reader to create meaning. Accordingly, vocabulary should be taught in the context of subject matter so that word meanings are related to each other and, where possible, to the prior experience of the learner. The knowledge position is taken in this chapter. It is consistent with schema theory in that it is an interactive approach by which new words are related to each other and to the learner's schemata.

In this chapter, you will have the opportunity to examine strategies by which new vocabulary is taught as a network of ideas—conceptual mapping, refocused semantic mappings, semantic feature analysis, and the Frayer model.

KINDS OF WORD MEANING

Words have different kinds of meanings. A word's denotive meaning refers specifically to a theory, a quality, an action, or a relationship. The teaching of vocabulary in the past often centered on this level of meaning: "Circle the word that matches the definition." However, from an interactive view of reading, it is more important to focus on the associative meanings of words (connotations). By way of example, the word *farm* may call to mind *field, row, fertilizer, plow, barn,* and much more. In this way a word is a central point for a chain of images. As indicated in Chapter 1, these complexes of associative meaning constitute a semantic field, which is important in making inferences and comprehending text.

In addition to representing objects and eliciting associations, words have the function of conveying the essential property of an object and relating it to other objects in a category. This is the categorical or conceptual meaning of a word. For example, the essential attribute of *pet* is domestication; of *fruit,* seed enclosure; of *myth,* conveyed picture of a shared ideal. Different things are categorized as equivalent or similar because they share essential properties. When new words and their referents are seen to belong to a known class or category, the reader generalizes from knowledge of the category to the new term. Thus, conceptual meanings become a primary basis for communication and learning. If, for example, an author refers to a particular role, and the reader does not grasp the general sense of the word *role* (expected action in an interactive situation of one in a given position), there is little comprehension. With knowledge of the general meaning of the term, the reader already knows a great deal about the role the author is talking about, even if the role is an unfamiliar one. The reader knows, for example, that the role is not dependent upon personality, that there are social consequences for departing from the expected action, and that others have a corresponding set of responses to the role. Knowledge of essential attributes of a category and the ability to generalize these properties to particular and novel words in the category make understanding of the new words possible.

ASSUMPTIONS ABOUT LEARNING WORDS

Newer techniques for teaching vocabulary are based upon four assumptions:

1. *Words are constantly being redefined.* By way of illustration, a very young reader understands *store* in terms of a precise object referent—a place where one can buy something—or perhaps in terms of the positive emotional connotations of toys and candy that *store* evokes. On the other hand, a mature reader has many concepts for *store,* including economic ideas of exchange (money, goods) or forms of exchange (capitalistic, cooperative). In other words, redefinition comes with developmental growth. One implication of this fact is that with very young children, vocabulary instruction should encourage developing affective associations and relating new terms to actual situations. When pupils begin to read in the content fields, the categorical meanings of words—abstract concepts—must receive attention. Indeed, the teacher must help pupils form hierarchies of connected categories.

2. *There are many meanings for a single word. Polysemy* refers to cases in which there are multiple meanings for a word. Texts with many polysemous words, especially seemingly simple and unambiguous words, create comprehension difficulties.

   The fact that there are so many meanings for a single word suggests that the teaching of vocabulary must help pupils see that it is not so important to learn *the* meaning of a word as to select the meaning required from several candidates. Inasmuch as context often determines the meaning of a word, the traditional practice of teaching context clues to word meaning is warranted. Pupils should practice using both syntactic and semantic cues in determining word meaning. It is helpful for pupils to learn how to use appositives and statements of contrast as clues to word meaning, together with guesses based on the situations described in the text.

   Active processing is desirable as a basis for increasing vocabulary and integrating word meaning with other words and the reader's schemata. Asking questions that demand applications of the new term in a variety of contexts is a technique for encouraging active processing. For example, in teaching the term *altercation,* you might ask: "Do you ever have altercations with your brother?" "Do you have

altercations with your antagonists?'' ''Would you invite antagonists
to your birthday party?''
3. *We should teach entire conceptual frameworks related to a word, not
   just the individual word.* Anderson and Freebody suggest that the
   child who knows the word *mast* is likely to have knowledge about
   sailing.[1] This general knowledge, not familiarity with the particular
   word *mast,* is what enables the child to understand text in which the
   word *mast* appears. The child who knows *mast* as part of a conceptual framework can also comprehend such statements as: ''We jibed
   suddenly, and the boom snapped across the cockpit.'' Instead of
   learning *mast* independently of such concepts as boat and sail, readers should learn sailing jargon in the context of sailing and sailboats.
   Trying to teach naive children a single sailing concept in isolation
   from related concepts (as is encouraged by authors of spelling work-
   books) is inefficient.

   One idea for teaching vocabulary so that it improves reading
   comprehension involves increasing the child's precision of word
   knowledge. Accordingly, words that share a common conceptual basis are taught together. For example, the words *hurl, thrust,* and
   nudge might be compared and contrasted with one another.
4. *When the conceptual meaning of a word is taught, the framework
   used should represent a hierarchy of terms.* Having said that concepts
   do not exist in isolation but as part of a set of related schemata, it is
   necessary to say something about how one decides upon the set to
   which the new word is to be linked.

   Often, in a reading selection, the set is already present in the
   narrative or in the circumstances described in connection with the
   new term. For example, the new term *plane* (a tool for smoothing
   wood) may appear in the context of a description of furniture-making
   along with words for related tools, purposes, standards, directions,
   and the like.

   At other times, the teacher must help pupils relate the new word
   to a hierarchy of related concepts. Some of the concepts should be
   superordinate (more abstract than the new word); others should be
   subordinate (instances of the target concept, perhaps); and others
   should be coordinate (of equal importance and degree of specificity).
   Coordinate terms may share many of the same attributes as the new
   term. By way of example, in teaching the meaning of *liquid,* coordinate terms to introduce might be *solid* and *gas.* Subordinate terms
   might be *water* and *oil.* Superordinate terms might be *states of matter*
   and *effects of heat.*

---

[1] Richard C. Anderson and Peter Freebody, ''Vocabulary Knowledge,'' in *Comprehension
and Teaching: Research Review,* ed. John T. Guthrie (Newark, Del.: International Reading
Association, 1981).

I suspect that many teachers will have difficulty in selecting sets of concepts that should be taught together. Textbooks are not always helpful in this regard. Most textbooks introduce one concept at a time and give only a denotive meaning for the terms followed by a simple example. The following vocabulary is meant to stimulate your own thinking about conceptual networks that might be appropriate for reading in your content field.

- *Art*—concepts related to materials, composition, and organization of elements, such as level, color, value, volume, depth, perspective, plane.
- *Math*—element, set, equality, sum, product, difference; logical concepts such as *is a member of, not, all, such that, if-then, or-and;* relations, functions, variables.
- *Physical science*—facts, hypotheses, principles, generalizations, laws, theories, models; energy, interactive particles and their organization; elements.
- *Biology*—species, genus, family, order, class, phylum, kingdom; evolution, inheritable variation, adaptation, natural selection, structural analysis, functional analysis; organization, organism, compound.
- *Sociology*—group, norm, role, status, institution, conformity, deviation, culture; value, need, conflict, change.
- *Economics*—land, population specialization, goods, service, exchange, market system, supply and demand, price, competition, monopoly, money, partnership, corporation, labor, wage, collective bargaining, conditions of work.

TEACHING VOCABULARY AS A NETWORK OF IDEAS

An illustration of how children can be helped to relate new vocabulary to both their background and other concepts has been provided by M. Buckley Hanf.[2] Hanf described a situation in which pupils were to read a selection from their science textbooks on the topic of black widow spiders. She first had pupils tell all they knew about the subject and then decide what they expected to find in the chapter. (She was, of course, activating and channeling purpose to guide the processing of text.) Next, she had pupils say what aspects of black widow spiders they expected the chapter to tell about and check the accuracy of their guesses by skimming the chapter. Headings and the labeling of sections also helped to identify categories for information. The categories became the start of a cognitive map, which was drawn on the chalkboard. With the larger view of the chapter in mind, pupils read for details and later restated details from memory (the recall of details from memory is important for monitoring

[2] M. Buckley Hanf, "Mapping: A Technique for Translating Reading into Thinking," *Journal of Reading* 14 (January 1971): 225–30.

comprehension). They also reread for poorly understood details. The pupils discussed new words met in the chapter, such as *abdomen, organs,* and *nocturnal,* by (a) referring to the examples given in the text, (b) asking each other for nonexamples of each term, (c) defining the terms in their own words, and (d) deciding where each new word should be placed on their map. Exhibit 6.1 shows the map. Note how it relates the topic to a hierarchy of concepts and details as well as relating the new words to the old.

Newer techniques for teaching vocabulary—semantic mapping, semantic feature analysis, the Frayer model, and contextual processing—are among the devices recommended for teaching the meaning of new words from an interactive perspective.

Exhibit 6.1   A Conceptual Map Relating New Vocabulary to Old

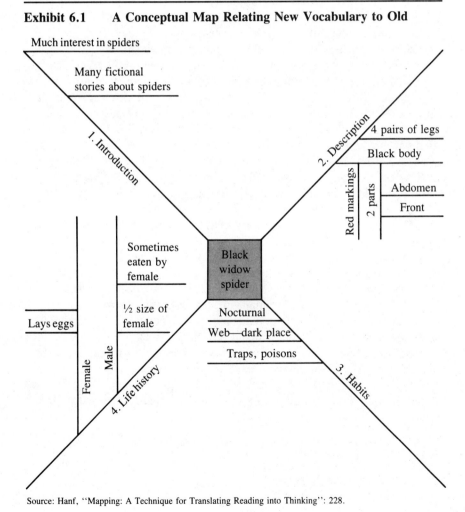

Source: Hanf, "Mapping: A Technique for Translating Reading into Thinking": 228.

SEMANTIC MAPPING

The semantic map was introduced in Chapter 1 as a tool for relating new concepts to a child's background knowledge. As a vocabulary-building device, mapping frequently is used to connect the conceptual meanings of new words to a hierarchical organization of concepts of schemata. One advantage of teaching words for their associative and categorical meanings—as opposed to their denotive meanings—is that it enhances recall. Whenever a particular concept in memory is activated, the whole structure of concepts with which it is associated is activated and becomes available for use in remembering and comprehending.

As mentioned, in the subject matter fields new terms should be related to other concepts at different levels in a structural hierarchy. Semantic maps make possible a graphic description of these levels. Exhibit 6.2, an example of a semantic map for *city*, illustrates how vocabulary terms are related at different levels of abstraction. This semantic map was used for comprehending a social studies assignment. Terms such as *city*, *state*, and *nation* were treated as labels for particular objects with whatever associations they brought to mind (denotive and associative meanings of the words). As information about a variety of cities accumulated, pupils abstracted and generalized their common properties and relationships (categorical or conceptual meanings of the words). The terms were then organized as shown on the map so that pupils could see how terms such as *nation, state, suburb,* and *city* are related to each other. Subsequently, in reading text in which these words appeared, the readers could draw upon their mental images of this map in constructing appropriate responses to the terms.

Student discussion is necessary in the preparation of a semantic map. Pupils should talk about the meanings and uses of new words, new meanings for old words, additional meanings for known words, and of course, the relationships among words.

Dale Johnson and others have introduced *refocused semantic maps* for helping pupils become familiar with text-specific meanings associated with a central concept.[3] The teacher initiates refocusing by centering on a textbook term that has a specialized meaning as well as several common associations. The pupils start the map with known examples, properties, and classes. After reading the selection, they revise the map to incorporate the new meanings. Exhibit 6.3 (p. 104) is an example of a refocused semantic map incorporating a text-specific meaning for the word *boom*.

---

[3] Dale D. Johnson, Susan Toms-Bronowski, and Susan D. Pittleman, *An Investigation of the Trends in Vocabulary Research and the Effects of Prior Knowledge on Instructional Strategies for Vocabulary Acquisition* (Madison: Wisconsin Center for Educational Research, University of Wisconsin, November 1981).

Exhibit 6.2   Semantic Map for City

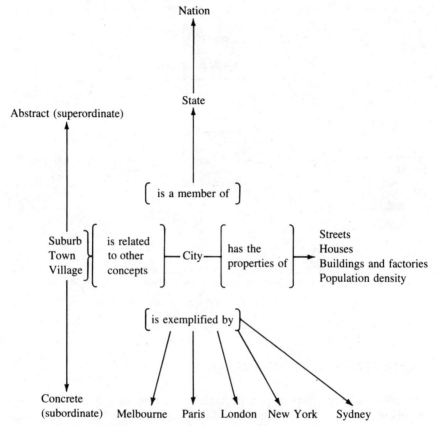

The map shows that a city has such features as streets, houses, buildings, factories, and population density. Examples of cities are Paris, New York, London, Melbourne, Sydney. *City* is also related to other schemata, such as *suburb, town,* and *village*. Finally, *city* can be subsumed under a more abstract concept, such as *state*, which in turn is subsumed under the concept *nation*. Thus, in the semantic map the upward direction is toward more abstract and more inclusive schemata and the downward direction is toward a more concrete and less inclusive level. But note that even though particular cities are exemplars of the concept *city*, they themselves are schemata with their own properties and relationships. For example, Paris has such features as the river Seine, Notre Dame cathedral, and the Eiffel Tower. Thus, the semantic map is a hierarchical organization of concepts or schemata within a reader's long-term memory.

The reader can draw upon the properties in his or her semantic map for constructing a response to the stimulus or printed word *city*. One response may be an image of a city. Whether an image forms of a particular city depends upon the information in the text. If the text provides constraining information for a particular city, the reader is likely to respond with the exemplar that fits the stated characteristics—provided, of course, that the exemplar is within the reader's memory. For example, given the sentence, "The city with its famous Eiffel Tower and historic buildings along the river Seine was lit up at night," the reader is likely to think of the city as Paris.

Source: H. Singer, "A Cognitive Framework for Comprehending Social Studies," in *The Nature of Teaching and Learning* (Victoria, Australia: Deakin University, 1982), p. 49.

Exhibit 6.3   Refocused Semantic Map for *Boom*

Text: During a thunderstorm a *boom* might become dislodged.

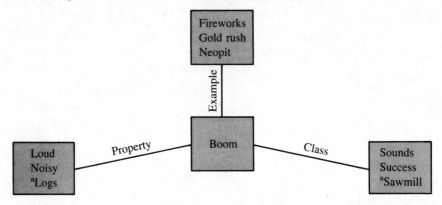

[a]Refocused concepts

Source: Dale D. Johnson, Susan Toms-Bronowski, and Susan D. Pittleman, *An Investigation of the Trends in Vocabulary Research and the Effects of Prior Knowledge on Instructional Strategies for Vocabulary Acquisition* (Madison: Wisconsin Center for Educational Research, University of Wisconsin), November 1981, p. 151.

SEMANTIC FEATURE ANALYSIS

Semantic feature analysis is a procedure for helping pupils to see how words within a category are alike and different and to relate the meanings of new words to prior knowledge. Vocabulary is presented in a logical manner:

1. A topic is selected.
2. Words related to the topic are listed in a column.
3. Features shared by some of the words are placed in a row.
4. Pupils put pluses and minuses in the resulting grid to indicate whether or not each word in the column has each feature listed in the row.
5. Pupils add words and features.

As pupils examine the patterns of pluses and minuses, they discover that no two words have identical patterns and hence that no two words have exactly the same meaning. Exhibit 6.4 is an example of a partially completed semantic feature analysis of shelters.

Ezra and Varda Stieglitz use semantic feature analysis as a culminating activity to a lesson when pupils have basic knowledge of a topic in a

Exhibit 6.4   Partial Semantic Feature Analysis of Shelters

Kinds of Shelter	Description of Shelters									Cost of Shelters			Things you find in Shelters			
	Large	Small	Exquisite	Lovely	Rustic	Simple	Spooky	Dilapidated	Open	Cheap	Expensive	Reasonable	Freezer	Bed	Wine cellar	Tools
Cabin	+	–	–	+			–	–								
Villa	–	+	+	–	–	–	–	–	–	–	+		+	+	+	?
Palace		+	+	–			–	–								
Shed		–	–	+			–	–								
Hovel	+	–	–	+	+	–	–	+	+	+	?		–	–	–	+
Barn	–	–		+			–	–								
Tent		–	–	+			–	–								
An old abandoned house		–	–	–			+	+								

Source: Dale D. Johnson, Susan Toms-Bronowski, and Susan D. Pittleman, *An Investigation of the Trends in Vocabulary Research and the Effects of Prior Knowledge on Instructional Strategies for Vocabulary Acquisition* (Madison: Wisconsin Center for Educational Research, University of Wisconsin, November 1981), p. 40.

Exhibit 6.5   Semantic Feature Analysis of Shapes

Shapes

	Four-sided	Curved or rounded	Line segment	All sides equal length	Right angle
Triangle	−	−	−	+	+
Rectangle	+	−	+	−	+
Parallelogram	+	−	+	+	+
Circle	−	+	−	−	−
Trapezoid	+	−	+	−	−
Semicircle	−	+	+	−	−
Square	+	−	+	+	+

Source: E. L. Stieglitz and V. S. Stieglitz, "Savor the Word to Reinforce Vocabulary in the Content Areas," *Journal of Reading* 25 (October 1981): 48.

content field.[4] Figure 6.5 is an example of a semantic feature analysis grid completed as a group activity in a math class under the direction of the Stieglitzes.

Disagreements about the qualities of concepts are opportunities for learning. One pupil who placed a plus next to *parallelogram* and beneath *sides equal* supported his choice by stating that the rhombus is a parallelogram that has four equal sides. Grids can be made more complex by replacing the + and − notations with numerical ratings (1–5). As a child's experience increases, the differentiations become more precise.

FRAYER MODEL

The Frayer model for attaining conceptual meanings of words was developed from work by Dorothy Frayer, Wayne Frederick, and Herbert

[4] E. L. Stieglitz and V. S. Stieglitz, "Savor the Word to Reinforce Vocabulary in the Content Areas," *Journal of Reading* 25 (October 1981): 46–51.

Klausmeir at the University of Wisconsin.[5] The model offers a systematic procedure for conceptualizing words. These are the steps in the model:

1. Discriminating the relevant qualities common to all instances of the concept. For example, the relevant attribute of *globe* is *spherical*.
2. Discriminating the relevant from the irrelevant properties of instances of the concept. For example, *large* or *small* is an irrelevant attribute for *globe*.
3. Providing an example of the concept, such as a classroom globe.
4. Providing a nonexample of the concept, such as a chart (non-spherical).
5. Relating the concept to a subordinate concept, such as *ball*.
6. Relating the concept to a superordinate term, such as *global*.
7. Relating the concept to a coordinate term, such as *map*.

In the event a concept cannot be defined by its relevant attributes, steps 1 and 2 are omitted and an antonym and a synonym are substituted for the defining relevant and irrelevant attributes (for example, for the concept *lovely,* a synonym might be *pretty;* an antonym, *ugly*).

The Frayer model is very useful in preparing pupils for a reading assignment. First, the teacher reviews an upcoming reading assignment to identify new words central to the topic. Together teacher and students supply the denotative meanings for the new words (usually the author states this meaning the first time the word is introduced, or it may appear in a glossary). Then, pupils try to provide both an example and a nonexample of the concept. The comparing of examples and nonexamples leads to identification of relevant and irrelevant attributes. I don't want to slight the difficulty that may occur in determining essential attributes. Sometimes there are overlapping attributes among members of a category rather than a single critical feature. Among democratic countries, for example, one country may have the features *a* and *b*; another, *b* and *c*; and a third, *c* and *d*. Members of categories with overlapping features have been described as sharing "family resemblances."[6]

Once the essential attribute is identified, pupils may supply coordinate, subordinate, and superordinate terms. Upon completion of this step, pupils are ready to read the assignment. When teaching children the critical attributes of categories, it is best to use the most perfect example

[5] Dorothy A. Frayer, Wayne C. Frederick, and Herbert J. Klausmeir, *A Schema for Testing the Level of Concept Mastery,* Working paper no. 16, (Madison: Wisconsin Research and Development Center for Cognitive Learning, University of Wisconsin, April 1969).

[6] Carolyn B. Mervis, "Category Structure and the Development of Categorization," in *Theoretical Issues in Reading Comprehension,* ed. R. J. Spiro et al., (Hillsdale, N.J.: Erlbaum, 1980), pp. 279–307.

(a robin, for instance, is a better example of a bird than a penguin). Poor examples often lead to an unreliable generalization or to a failure to generalize at all. Further, a category is not always defined by a perceptual attribute, but sometimes by a function—what it can be used for and what it can do.

As an illustration of children's conceptual development, consider the story of children playing a game of "odd out," where they were to find one of three items that "didn't belong." Adults were puzzled why, when given the words *dog, car,* and *cat,* the children selected *cat* as odd. Interviews revealed that the children regarded *car* and *dog* as the only two items that required a license.

Charles Peters compared the reading comprehension of pupils who used conventional social studies textbooks and pupils instructed according to the Frayer model.[7] Both good and poor readers who used materials organized in accordance with the Frayer model comprehended better than comparable pupils who used materials with the conventional features of textbooks. The textbook materials in Peters's study differed from those following the Frayer model in these ways:

Textbook	*Frayer model*
Definition of term and example	Definition and example
No nonexample	Defining attribute
	Nonexample
Concept is introduced in	Concept is related to
context of historical period	superordinate, coordinate, and
	subordinate terms

Peters also tried to relate key terms to the background of pupils. For example, in including the concept *diplomacy* in the context of settling a territorial dispute between nations, he referred to the territorial disputes of street gangs—but only if the pupils had a schema for street gang warfare.

CONTEXTUAL PROCESSING

It's almost a platitude to say that the meaning of a word depends upon its context. However, context has many dimensions. The situation in which reading occurs is context. The reader as a person with prior experience constitutes context. So, too, does the purpose for reading. The schema for the work as a whole—exposition, narration—is a contextual variable

---

[7] Charles Peters, *A Comparison Between the Frayer Model of Concept Attainment and the Textbook Approach to Concept Attainment* (Madison: Wisconsin Research and Development Center for Cognitive Learning, University of Wisconsin, February 1974).

that will influence the meaning the reader gives to words (one interprets *check* differently when reading an auto mechanic's manual than when reading a historical novel).

Narrower contexts for determining word meaning are paragraphs and adjacent sentences. Techniques for determining word meaning in these narrow contexts are presented in the following discussion.

A study by two Dutch investigators—M. Van Daalen-Kapteijns, and M. Elshout-Mohr—throws light upon the process by which word meaning is derived from narrow context clues.[8] In their study, the investigators asked pupils to find the meaning of unfamiliar words such as *kolper* from serially presented sentences similar to the following:

1. When you're used to a broad view, it is quite depressing when you come to live in a room with one or two *kolpers* fronting a courtyard.
2. He virtually always studied in the library, as at home he had to work by artificial light all day because of those *kolpers*.
3. During a heat wave a lot of people all of a sudden wanted to have *kolpers,* so the sales of sun blinds then reached a peak.

Perhaps you derived from the first sentence a hypothesized schema for *kolper* and used this schema to fill in additional information about kolpers.

Most students hypothesize from the first sentence that *kolpers* are windows. In order to understand what sort of window a kolper is, one must reformulate the sentences so that they relate to the meaning of the new word. For example, sentence 2 may be reformulated to read "Having kolpers in a house means having artificial light on all day." Also, one must transform the reformulated sentence into something that fits the hypothesized schema. Such a transformation for sentence 2 might be "Kolpers transmit little light."

Good comprehenders make more substantive transformations than poor comprehenders. For example, for sentence 3 a typical response from poor comprehenders is "Kolpers are much asked for during a heat wave" (a literal reformation), while good comprehenders say something like, "Kolpers have a cooling effect" (a generalized reformation).

Support for an interactive model for teaching word meanings in context has been found by Joan Gipe.[9] She reasons that a familiar context will activate a learner's "old information" or schema and that the new mean-

---

[8] M. Van Daalen-Kapteijns, M. Elshout-Mohr, "The Acquisition of Word Meaning as a Cognitive Learning Process," *Journal of Verbal Learning and Verbal Behavior* 20 (1981): 386–99.
[9] J. P. Gipe, "Investigating Techniques for Teaching Word Meanings," *Reading Research Quarterly* 14, no. 4 (1978–1979): 624–44.

ing will then be assimilated. By relating the new word to an existing schema, the learner is more likely to retain the meaning of the new word.

Gipe's interactive context method for teaching word meaning requires that pupils read a three-sentence passage in which each sentence uses the target word in a defining context. Simple sentence structures and common words are used in the sentences in order to make the context familiar. Pupils respond in writing after reading the sentences, giving a word or phrase from their own experience that defines the new word. An example adapted from Gipe's materials appears below:

The *brute* kicked the dog and hit the owner on the nose.

Any person who acts cruel to anybody or to anything is acting like a brute.

A brute is a person who is very mean. Write down something that a brute might do at the dinner table.

Third- and fifth-graders comprehended new words better when taught by the interaction context method than when taught by any of the following methods:

1. An *associative method* by which they paired a new word with a familiar synonym or brief definition. Students were told: "Memorize the list of word pairs. Try to write this list again without looking at it."

   Brute—cruel, mean person
   Graphite—pencil
   Colossal—large
   Wretched—unhappy

2. A *category method* whereby pupils added to a list of words fitting a general category. Each list contained a new word and three familiar words. Pupils added words from their own backgrounds and recategorized a random list composed of previously learned words:

Bad people	*Things you can write with*
Mean	Pencil
Cruel	Graphite
Brute	Marker
Robber	Chalk

Words meaning big	*The way you look when unhappy*
Huge	Wretched
Large	Sad
Giant	Frowning
Colossal	Miserable

3. A *dictionary method* whereby pupils look up designated words, wrote the definitions, and then wrote sentences containing each new word.

Although each method benefited vocabulary development, the interactive context method was better than other methods for pupils at both grade levels and for both good and poor readers. Asking pupils to apply a new word meaning to their own experience was valuable in all instances.

Activity 6.1   Determining Word Meaning from Context Clues

Typically, three types of context clues are taught in order to help readers derive the meaning of unfamiliar words—*direct explanation, appositive,* and *contrast.* Examples of these clues appear below. Study them and then see if you can use such clues in guessing the meaning of uncommon words. If you determine the meaning of a word and you want to remember it, make a statement (written or oral) in which you use the word in connection with some aspect of your life.

Direct Explanation
Volatility refers to the ease with which a liquid vaporizes, becoming a gas.
The lumber industry hires *bushers*—persons who trim the limbs and large knots from felled trees.
Appositive
The *swizzle,* a drink made with crushed ice, rum, and bitters, is popular in the tropics.
The *sycamore,* a shade tree with an edible fruit, is mentioned often in the Scriptures.
Contrast
The value of most furniture decreases as soon as it is sold, but antique furniture *appreciates* with age.
It was never seen at the apex; on the other hand, its orbit was viewed at *perigee.*

Select the answer that best defines the italicized word.

1. In contrast to the vigor of Edith, Viola was characterized by her *evanescence.*
a. enduring quality
b. fleeting quality
2. Instead of hardening the skin, it was an *emollient.*
a. softening application
b. stiffening application
3. He wasn't a miser, but a *prodigal.*
a. given to extravagance
b. an extraordinary person
4. Humorously, his nose was a *proboscis,* a long flexible snout.
a. trunk of an elephant
b. wings of an insect

Should you want to remember a new word from this exercise, use it in a statement about something related to your personal life.

Activity 6.2   Developing Conceptual Vocabulary

Exhibit 6.6 is an incomplete semantic feature analysis grid for musical instruments. If this topic is appropriate for your pupils, you may wish to have them add more words and features and then indicate which features apply to each word. If the topic is not appropriate, select a topic from a textbook used by your pupils. Together you and your pupils determine the instances and the qualities or attributes to place on the grid. Complete the grid by placing + or − in the appropriate squares. Completion of the grid should involve discussion that will illuminate the changing conceptual meanings of words. As jazz symphonies and other musical innovations occur, there are corresponding changes in the meanings of words for musical instruments.

Exhibit 6.6   Incomplete Semantic Feature Analysis of Musical Instruments

| | Description | | | | Musical quality | | | | | Musical group | | |
	Wind	Strings	Percussion	Large size	Deep tone	Low pitch	Soft	Shrill	Mellow	Marching band	Orchestra	Wind ensemble
Violin		+										
Trumpet	+	−									+	−
Piano	−	+	+	+								
Bass					+	+						
Drum											+	

SUMMARY

This chapter emphasizes an interactive approach to vocabulary development by teaching new words in the context of subject matter and related words. It includes suggestions for helping readers relate new terms to their own backgrounds. Chief among recommended teaching and learning strategies are cognitive mapping, semantic mapping, semantic feature analysis, the Frayer model, inference of word meanings from context clues, and use of new vocabulary in a variety of contexts. The techniques emphasize concern for active processing of new vocabulary so that vocabulary development enhances reading comprehension, not just word knowledge.

Activity 6.3　Applying the Frayer Model

Select a key term from a textbook you are using and then complete each of the following steps:

1. *Example.* Provide an instance of the concept.
2. *Nonexample.* Provide a noninstance of the concept.
3. *Relevant attribute.* Name the relevant attribute (or attributes) or the defining properties for the term selected.
4. *Irrelevant attribute.* List any attribute that is associated with the concept but is not indispensable in identifying whether something or someone is or is not an instance of the concept.
5. *Subordinate term.* Name a more specific part or illustration of the term you have selected.
6. *Superordinate term.* Name a term that refers to a related concept (principle, generalization, theory) that is more general and encompassing than the term you have selected.
7. *Coordinate term.* Name a term that often appears in the same context as your selected term and that is neither subordinate nor superordinate to your term. The coordinate may share some of the same attributes.

This activity can be used either as a preteaching vocabulary lesson before a selection is read, or as a summary lesson after reading.

You may decide to try something more ambitious—to encourage pupils to use the Frayer model on their own. An approach to such a goal is to give many opportunities for pupils to determine relevant attributes, irrelevant attributes, examples, and nonexamples and to select related hierarchical terms for familiar concepts.

Useful Reading

Freedman, G., and E. G. Reynold. "Enriching Basal Reader Lessons with Semantic Webbing." *Reading Teacher* 36, no. 6 (1980); 677–84.

Humes, A. *Requirements for Vocabulary Development Instruction.* Technical note #3–76–08. Los Alamitos, Calif.: Southwest Regional Laboratory, 1976.

Humes, A. *The Use of Concept-Learning Techniques in Vocabulary Development.* Technical note #3–77–06. Los Alamitos, Calif.: Southwest Regional Laboratory, 1977.

McCullough, C. "Context Aids in Reading." *Reading Teacher* 11, no. 2 (1968): 225–29.

Mezynski, Karen. "Issues Concerning the Acquisition of Knowledge: Effect of Vocabulary Training on Reading Comprehension." *Review of Educational Research* 53, no. 2 (Summer 1983): 253–79.

Tennyson, Robert D., and Ok-Choon Park. "The Teaching of a Concept: A Review of Instructional Design Research Literature." *Review of Educational Research* 50, no. 1 (Spring 1980): 55–70.

7 Improving Comprehension of Sentences

Overview

Experienced teachers know what sentences are difficult for pupils to understand. They know, for example, that pupils have more problems with the passive patterns (*It was seen by Bill*) than the more common noun-verb-object pattern (*Bill saw it*). Other troublesome patterns are appositives with commas—*Betty, my sister, came*—and clauses as subjects—*What you think is your business.*

It's not only the pattern that signals ease or difficulty in interpreting sentences; difficulty is often associated with pronouns and sentences that require a referent (anaphora), particular connectives, punctuation, and figurative language. The fact that sentences are not isolated links but can only be understood in light of the preceding sentences and, in some cases, the subsequent sentences is important.

This chapter will illustrate the types of reading problems that frequently arise with sentences, give reasons for the difficulties, and describe strategies for helping pupils overcome them.

114

SENTENCE PATTERNS THAT REQUIRE TRANSFORMING

You might recall from Chapter 5 that good readers differ from poor readers in their ability to transform or reformulate sentences into more meaningful patterns. The importance of transformation was recognized by Noam Chomsky, who drew attention to the difference between surface syntactic structure, one of the innumerable forms in which an idea may appear in print, and deep syntactic structure, which reflects in a simpler form the basic idea itself.[1] (For example, *I wrote a letter to the president* and *I wrote to the president a letter* both say *I wrote the president a letter.*)

Consequently, we now believe that sentence comprehension involves translation from surface to deep syntactic structure. In some sentences, however, there is a close match between surface and deep structure; little transformation is required. A simple sentence such as *The boy hit the ball* has the same pattern at both levels of structure. Other sentences require that readers carry out special operations in order to make the transformation from surface to deep structure. Consider the example *We elected Mary president.* The reader must insert the idea *Mary is president* into the basic sentence *We elected Mary.*

The following types of frequently appearing sentences present difficulties because their surface structures differ from their deep structures. Each of these types of sentences requires a transformation:

1. *Passive voice.* Comprehension of sentences written in the passive voice can be difficult, because the passive frequently disrupts the correlation between the succession of words and the succession of events. The passive is made up of a form of *be* (children often use *got* as the passive form) and the past participle of the principal verb (*The game is played by Tim*). The passive is produced by inverting basic word order (noun-verb-object), and introducing a form of *be:*
   Tabby was given milk by Meg.
   Milk was given Tabby by Meg.
   Her cat was called Tabby.
   These passive forms can be transformed into the simple active form by the addition of an actor and an action:
   Meg gave Tabby milk.
   Meg calls her cat Tabby.
   In transforming passive sentences, the key question is "Who is the recipient of the action?" Pupils need to know how to remove the inversion. To this end, a teacher may first model the transforming process. A number of transformations may be given and the pupils

---

[1] Noam Chomsky, *Syntactic Structures* (The Hague: Mouton, 1957).

may derive from these examples their own rule for making transformations. Later, pupils may be given simple sentences and asked to produce passive forms from them. Or pupils may play a game in which they challenge each other in recognizing the passive form for basic sentences:

Larry hit the ball.
  a.   The ball was hit by Larry.
  b.   Larry was hit by the ball.
  c.   Larry the ball hit.

Mature readers may want to discuss why writers use the passive voice. They may be led to see how it modifies the topic of a sentence. Instead of known information being presented at the beginning of a sentence and new information at the end, for example, the passive may be used to relegate the known to the object. This shift in order removes attention from the actor and emphasizes the content. Sometimes the author shows an unwillingness to accept responsibility for the idea by using the passive (*It is believed* versus *I believe*).

2.   *Sentences with relative clauses.* Comprehension difficulties sometimes occur when the subordinate clause immediately follows the main clause and when the subordinate clause is embedded in the main clause. For example, *The girl saw the boy who caught the fish* must be transformed into two sentences: (1) *The girl saw the boy* and (2) *The boy caught the fish. Who* does not refer to *girl* but to *boy.* In helping pupils be aware of the need for making transformations in sentences with clauses, give pupils sentences that have relative clauses and ask them to identify the sentences involved.

Relative clauses that make use of the words *which* and *who* may cause confusion. This is true at least when it is not clear which element of the sentence is being referred to by *which* or *who.* For example, consider the sentence: *The painting, which Otterson drew and which attracted so much negative comment, received a prize at the exhibition.* In comprehending this sentence, one must inhibit a quick decision about the meaning and join together widely separated components into a single sense: *The painting won a prize. Otterson drew the painting.*

3.   *Reverse ordering of events.* Sometimes the succession of words in a sentence is not the same as the natural succession of events. *I played after I did my homework* means that I did my homework earlier and played afterward. The reversal in temporal order requires that the reader make a mental transformation. Consider how a child might transform the following question to conform with temporal order: *How many marbles did Susan end up with if she found two marbles and she started out with three?*

4. *Conflict in semantic structure.* The Russian psychologist Alexander Luria refers to a class of comprehension difficulties that arise because of discrepancy between surface and deep *semantic* (not *syntactical*) structure of sentences.[2] Semantic inversions are not easy to understand directly. They often involve mixing something negative with something positive—*She was the last of the group* (negative) *with regard to independence* (positive). The statement means that she was first with regard to dependence. Thus, in order to understand a semantic inversion, we really must transfer the sentence into its opposite. Sentences requiring replacing a negative with an affirmative are *Which of these is less empty?* (*less empty* means *more full*) and *It's not likely that I won't go.* Try asking pupils to create semantically inverted sentences for their companions to transform. Here are some examples:

I'm not unhappy.

There is no one who can't go.

Don't call me if he doesn't come.

COMPREHENDING ANAPHORIC RELATIONSHIPS

Anaphora refers to the use of expressions that link sentences, such as a pronoun linked to a noun. The resulting relationship is called an anaphoric relationship. By way of example: *The dog barked. It was trying to get attention. It* is related to *dog* in the previous sentence.

Although pronouns are frequently used as substitutes for nouns or groups of nouns, a pro-verb (not proverb) can be linked to a verb: *Tom washed the windows. He did it very quickly. It* is linked to the verb *washed.*

Pro-sentences are words that substitute for previous sentences: *The highest learning rates were achieved in a program which used poor assessment techniques and had a large number of drop-outs. This makes it impossible to determine the impact of instruction itself. This* is a pro-sentence referring to the previous sentence in its entirety. Sometimes the anaphoric term does not appear in an adjacent sentence but five or six sentences later. Also, it may appear before the word it will replace: *Now that you've burned this, we don't have enough mix to make another cake.* In this example, the referent *this* precedes its reference *cake.* Such backward-leading relationships are called *cataphoric.* Cataphoric relations become clear as more of the text appears.

[2] Alexander R. Luria, *Language and Cognition,* ed. James V. Wertsch (New York: John Wiley & Sons, 1981).

"Invisible" anaphora involved elliptical sentences:

"Is Bill going to enter the contest?" asked Joe.
"I don't know," answered Mike.

In this example, the reader must supply the invisible anaphoric terms:

"I don't know if Bill is going to enter the contest."

Other examples of invisible anaphora are:

If Rex told Joe he would ride, he will. (He will *ride*.)
If you want him to sell the ticket, he will. (He will *sell the ticket*.)

Invisible anaphora require that the reader infer the words that will complete the relationship.

One final kind of anaphora involves the substituting of a superordinate word for a word lower in a hierarchical relationship or the reverse:

Will you feed *Oscar and Harriet?*
Reptiles have to eat, you know.

"Do you want to see the biggest *mammals?*" asked Kay.
"I love *whales,*" replied Sandy.

Anaphora and Inferencing

As with other aspects of comprehending text, the most important factor in recognizing antecedents is the ability to make inferences about the content. For example, in the sentences *A Scot loaned me money. They are really thrifty people,* one must infer that *they* refers to the class *Scots* on the basis of the lexical term *Scot* and a schema for loaning money and thrift. That is, the meaning of an anaphoric relationship is determined as much by the background experience of the reader as by linguistic conventions indicating antecedents, such as the way number and gender provide clues to the meaning of pronouns.

Teaching Strategies for Comprehending Anaphoric Relationships

Typically pupils are only 60 to 80 percent accurate in recognizing antecedents. Improvement can occur through instruction, but the improvement will only be noted when the readers are interpreting word relations within familiar contexts. Peggy Moberly and Dianne Monson, for example, have had success in teaching fifth-graders four kinds of anaphoric ties in immediate, mediated, and remote positions.[3]

Strategies for helping pupils interpret anaphora include metacognitive awareness, question probing, antecedent matching exercises, and rule generation.

1. *Metacognitive awareness.* Many pupils have never thought about anaphoric relations and their ability to interpret them. One suggestion for increasing pupils' consciousness of their ability to interpret anaphora is to take a selection with which pupils are familiar and ask them to identify all words that substitute for other words. Once the replacement words have been identified, pupils should name the antecedent of each. The relations identified can then be classified by pupils into such categories as pronouns, pro-verbs, pro-sentences, and superordinate terms.

   The reverse of this activity is also recommended: Here, the teacher first defines the categories of anaphora and then asks pupils to find instances of these categories in the selection.

2. *Question probing.* The following table illustrates questions for helping readers interpret different kinds of anaphora in sentences of varying complexity.

Category	Example	Probe
Pronoun (easy)	Terry looked up. "I will try," he said. "Good!" said Grandpa. "We will both try."	Name the person or persons who will try.
(difficult)	"T'was at the royal feast, one Persia won By Philip's warlike son Aloft in awful state The God-like hero sat On his imperial throne.	Who sat on the throne? What is his name? (Answer: Alexander)

---

[3] Peggy Moberly and Dianne L. Monson, *Effect of Instruction on Fifth Graders' Comprehension of Anaphoric Structures* (Unpublished paper, University of Washington, Seattle, 1981).

Category	Example	Probe
Pro-verb (easy)	Joe made a space helmet. So did Mike.	What did Mike do?
(difficult)	They claim that Beverly Hills is the wealthiest city in the world. She turned to the big man. "What do you think?" "I wouldn't know," said the big man. "It may be so."	What may be so?
Pro-sentence (easy)	No matter where the brothers went, they always went together. That's why it was so strange to see him there alone.	Why was it strange to see him alone?
(difficult)	The guilty soul of a murderer cannot keep its own secret. It is false to itself or rather it feels an irresistible impulse to be true to itself. The honest heart was not made for the residence of such an inhabitant. That is why it must be confessed.	What must be confessed? Why?

Category	Example	Probe
Superordinate term (easy)	At the beginning of our story about the finch, the little bird was still gray.	What color was the finch?
(difficult)	Are fleets and armies necessary to a work of love and reconciliation? Have we shown ourselves to be so unwilling to be reconciled that force must be called in to win back our lives? Let us not deceive ourselves, sir. These are the implements of war and subjugation— the last arguments to which kings resort.	Name the implements of subjugation.

3. *Antecedent matching.* One way to carry out antecedent matching is to place numbers over linked terms found in a familiar passage. Pupils write the same number over the words that are linked in an anaphoric relationship.

　　　　　　　　　　(1)
Did you know that a beaver looks something like a big

　　　(1)　　　(2)　　　　　(2)
rat? His front teeth are so big they can cut down small

　　　(1)　　　(3)　　　　　　　　(3)
trees. His back feet are big and look like they might

　　　　　　(1)　(4)　　　　　　　(4)
be a duck's feet. His coat is brown and from it we make
coats and hats.

4. *Rule generation.* An excellent activity is to engage pupils in formulating rules or strategies for interpreting the anaphoric relations they know. The rules may not be stated exactly as you or I would state

them, but the idea may be the same. The following are examples of rules or strategies for determining particular anaphoric relations:

a. *The number-and-gender strategy*
Sue and Ann went to the beach. *They* like to swim. Lois saw Steve. *She* saw *him* on the corner. (In finding the referent for a pronoun, look for an antecedent that has the same number or gender.)

b. *The using-your-own-experience strategy*
He went from home to school. *It* was closed. (*It* must be the school because you know that schools are more likely to be closed than homes.)

c. *The same-subject strategy*
Frank opened the door for Fred. *He* was then on *his* way. (*Frank* is the subject in the first sentence, so the subject in the subsequent sentence is likely to be the same—Frank.)

d. *The receiving strategy*
The principal spoke to the nurse and then asked for Mary. *She* wasn't in her room. (The last-mentioned person or thing in the previous sentence is likely to be the antecedent for the anaphoric term in the second sentence—not the nurse, but Mary.)

AIDS TO UNDERSTANDING SENTENCE RELATIONS

Relationships among sentences are both explicit and implicit. The latter can only be understood by the drawing of inferences, which in turn depends upon background knowledge of the context. Explicitly encoded relationships are signaled by a number of conventional aids—typographical cues, relational terms, and guide words. Teaching pupils how to use these aids is beneficial—especially for the poorer readers, who do not have well-established schemata for interpreting related sentences.

Typographical Aids

A great variety of type styles and punctuation is used in reading selections. Comic strips use drawings of balloons to indicate direct quotes; technical writers may use quotation marks to indicate the ironic use of a word. Whatever materials your pupils are reading should be previewed for type style and punctuation. Pupils should discuss how the author signals upcoming ideas of importance, shows how ideas are related, and clarifies meaning through the use of typographical aids. Among the more common punctuation devices are the colon, semicolon, and comma.

The colon indicates a two-part idea. The first part is an introduction to get attention, and the second part is either a summation or an elaboration. The semicolon tells the reader that two closely related ideas are in the same sentence. The second idea may be a detail that clarifies or adds emphasis. Although the comma has many uses, its use in signaling a series of items or events is especially important, letting readers know they should slow down in their reading in order to grasp each of the separate concepts.

Frequently in children's literature elipses (. . .) signify a pause or interruption; dashes (—) and parentheses indicate an aside comment or a less essential addition to the sentence. The multiple meanings of these and other punctuation marks can be taught in the contexts of reading and writing. Having pupils write messages to each other in which they use different punctuation and type style is a case in point.

Connectives as Guide Words

Guide words not only link ideas together, they show *how* the ideas are related. They are signs that let the reader know what's coming up. To see how they work, consider these sentences: *They were fed, clothed, observed for days, and then sent to their new home in apparently fine shape. Each was back in the juvenile hall within the month.*

As you can see, the last sentence just doesn't go with the previous sentence. The transition is too abrupt. In order to warn that the second sentence will call for a change in thought, add the guide word *yet* between *shape* and *each.* Now reread the passage. You will note how much easier it is to relate the final opposing idea to the previous thought.

A technique for sensitizing pupils to the significance of guide words is to discuss how changing the guide word changes the meaning of sentences such as the following:

Joe stopped	when	Meg kept on running.
	and	
	yet	
I will stay	but	you will go.
	or	
	so	
She eats	where	he cleans the dishes.
	if	
	while	

The guide word most frequently used to signal cause and effect relations is *because.* In the sentence *I brought an umbrella because it is going to rain,* the effect precedes the cause. Other connectives link a preceding causal idea to a subsequent effect (*It was snowing, so I put on snow tires.*)

Words such as *since, if, as,* and *for* often signal causal relations: *If you can't count on the family* (cause), *you may want to get additional resources* (effect). Conclusions or summaries related to previously mentioned causes are signaled by the guide words *consequently, therefore, thus, hence,* and *accordingly.*

Ideas are linked to time by guide words like *when, until, meanwhile, before, always, following, finally, during,* and *initially.* For example, note how *after* and *immediate* relate time in this sentence: *If problems surface in the weeks after the treatment, you have to take immediate action.* As indicated earlier, when the order of time cues does not correspond to the actual order of events, a transformation is required.

One technique for teaching guide words for time is to ask pupils to write directions for doing something they know how to do (making fudge or tying shoes) using a list of guide words you have supplied. Another technique is to use exercises in which pupils select the appropriate cue word—*Steve studied (after, before, until) he awakened.*

I want to reiterate that the teaching of guide words is not *the* answer to the problem of comprehending relationships among ideas in sentences. Guide words are aids, especially for poorer readers; however, identification of cause and effect, understanding of sequential relations, and drawing of conclusions rest more upon one's having appropriate schemata for the content of the material than upon one's ability to interpret surface clues.

ANALOGIES, METAPHORS, SIMILES, AND OTHER COIKs[4]

The idea of using the known to comprehend the unknown takes many forms. An author of a naturalistic selection may introduce an unfamiliar topic by showing its similarity to a familiar idea. Perhaps you recall being introduced to the flow of electrical current by an analogy to waterflow. In the aesthetic area, it is common to put two known elements, which are only remotely related, together in order to create a fresh meaning or image: "All the world's a stage, and all the men and women merely players."

Using Analogy as a Bridge

What do you think of doing when your pupils lack knowledge of the topic they are to read about? Your answer probably is that it is necessary to increase the experiential background of the pupils with respect to the

---

[4] *COIK* stands for "clear only if known."

unfamiliar topic. That answer is acceptable. However, a less direct approach may also be of value. It may be that the pupils already know something that will help them in learning the topic. Making an analogy between what they already know and the new topic may be an effective teaching and learning strategy.

David Hayes and Robert Tierney have presented evidence in support of analogy as a device for activating schemata and increasing reading comprehension of unfamiliar material.[5] They had three groups of pupils read newspaper articles about an unfamiliar topic—the game of cricket. Pupils in one group read a baseball passage (familiar material to activate relevant information) and then read about cricket in a selection in which analogies such as the following had been embedded:

Unlike baseball, cricket always has two batsmen in play at the same time.

The center of activity is an area in the middle of the field called a pitch, *which corresponds to the infield in baseball.*

Pupils in another group read the unfamiliar material with analogies but without the preliminary reading of the article about baseball. A third group read the baseball articles and then the material about cricket without the embedded analogies.

Those pupils given the knowledge-evoking information (the baseball article) as well as the embedded analogies showed the highest comprehension of the new material. Those who were given the knowledge-evoking article but not the embedded analogies comprehended the new material better than those who did not have the background text.

Few teachers will use analogy as the investigators did. The use of a semantic map as described in Chapters 1 and 6 offers a more practical approach. The map can easily be adapted to making an analogy between a known and an unknown topic. Often a coordinate term in the map will be familiar enough to use for comparison with the new term.

Teachers also may create their own introduction to unfamiliar material by suggesting relevant personal analogies ("Before you read this chapter, imagine yourself as a light beam whose reflection is being measured") and by making direct analogies ("Photosynthesis in plants (new content) is like eating in people. What does eating do for people?"). The important points are that (a) the pupil must have the knowledge structure for the element to which the new information is to be related and (b) this structure must be activated.

[5] David A. Hayes and Robert J. Tierney, "Developing Readers' Knowledge Through Analogy," *Reading Research Quarterly* 17, no. 2 (1982): 256–80.

Comprehending Figures of Speech

The interpretation of metaphors, similes, and hyperbole involves conno-
tation:

* You're so disagreeable, your own shadow won't keep you company.
  (hyperbole)
* She's as busy as a bee. (simile)
* She's a bee in her activity as well as in her sting. (metaphor)

Central to the comprehension of figures of speech is the understanding that the literal interpretation of words won't always work. There is
more meaning than what the words actually say. Exercises to introduce
pupils to this prerequisite may take these forms:

1. Matching a literal meaning with a figurative expression.

   Roberta is fragile.   Roberta is like:
                          fine china.
                          rough diamonds.
                          bubble gum.

2. Rewriting literal statements.
   Pupils may, for example, rewrite the sentence *He loses his temper
   quickly* as *He's a firecracker* or *He's got a hair trigger.*

3. Interpreting figurative language.

   It's easier to interpret similes than metaphors. Unlike metaphors,
   similes make an explicit reference and signal that a comparison is being
   made with such words as *like* and *as.* Indeed, one way to interpret a
   metaphor is to first transform it into a simile:

   This revolving door policy won't work.
   The policy is like a revolving door.
   The policy permits a problem to reappear.

   According to schema theory, people interpret figurative language
   when they have a schema for each of the items compared. To understand
   the sentence *Fred is an encyclopedia,* one must have a schema for *Fred*
   (male person and other associations) and a schema for *encyclopedia*
   (something that is filled with facts, has knowledge separated into compart-
   ments, is heavy, has many pages, and other connotations).
   In comparing the two schema, readers will find that not all parts
   match. They must ask, "What aspects of both schema are the same?"
   Both Fred and the encyclopedia are sources of a fund of information, but
   number of pages is not a common element.

Schemata or comparisons that don't match are called *tensions*. Usually, the literal element being discussed (called the *topic*) is compared with a figurative item (called the *vehicle,* or the thing to which the topic is compared). The commonality between the literal topic and the figurative vehicle is the *ground.*

In teaching, it is important to give pupils opportunities to identify the topic and the vehicle, to figure out the ground, and to recognize tension. Comprehension depends upon the pupils' having schemata for both topic and vehicle. Consider a remark attributed to Boswell: "Well," said Dr. Johnson, "we had a good talk." "Yes, sir," said Boswell, "you tossed and gored several persons." Only someone with schemata for bulls and matadors could appreciate the comment.

It may be necessary to help some pupils recognize that writers sometimes represent inanimate objects or ideas as persons or as having the qualities of persons. Pupils should be asked to identify words that are actually only associated with living things but that in figurative expression may be attributed to the inanimate. (*The* patient *stone* nestled *against the tree.*) Children learn to interpret figurative language by constructing sentences that transfer human qualities—dreaming, smiling, laughing—to objects in nature. (*The sun* stuck his tongue out *before* hiding *in the night.*)

The problem of when to take a statement figuratively rather than literally is resolved through context. The expression *He put his sights on the wrong star* should be read literally in a story about a navigator. In the context of a tale of a wayward son, the reader would properly regard it as metaphorical.

As an instructional activity, you may wish to have pupils describe the contexts in which statements such as the following would be literal and then describe the contexts in which they should be comprehended as metaphorical:

Let sleeping dogs lie.
You've got egg on your face.
Voters sent a message to Congress.
She put all her eggs in one basket.

Activity 7.1   Using Sentence Anagrams for Improving Reader Comprehension

---

Background

The technique of sentence-combining can be used with many of the problems identified in this chapter—transformations, anaphora, guide words, figurative language. Basically, the sentence anagram task is an organizational activity that calls for applying a grouping strategy. Phyllis Weaver has dem-

---

Activity 7.1   *(Continued)*

---

onstrated the value of this activity.[6] The Weaver procedure for solving sentence anagrams resulted in dramatic increases in reading comprehension. The program itself took fifteen minutes a day, three days a week, for five weeks.

Weaver taught children to solve sentence anagrams of increasing length in relatively less time by "chunking" words into higher-order units. Pupils were taught to use a word-grouping strategy by which they arranged words systematically into phrases and then arranged the phrases into sentences. The strategy called for first identifying the action word or verb and then asking a series of questions to group the remaining words and to relate the groups to the verb. Exhibit 7.1 shows the general structure of the word-grouping strategy for constructing an array of words into declarative sentences. The actions are shown in rectangles and the decisions in diamonds.

Pupils were taught to perform the actions shown in the rectangles and how to monitor their actions by asking and answering the questions shown in the diamonds. The strategy assumes knowledge of several concepts— *action words; wh* questions (who? what? where?); *sensibleness* (does the grouping make sense, both semantically and syntactically?).

Once a pupil had solved a sentence anagram using the word-grouping strategy, a time element was introduced. Time was recorded and pupils were encouraged to decrease the time needed to solve sentence anagrams. When pupils could solve anagrams of a given length within sixty to ninety seconds, longer sentence anagrams were introduced.

In Weaver's study, vocabulary was no higher than second-grade level, and punctuation was omitted. Also, Weaver worked with individual pupils.

General Plan for the Activity

Try teaching a modified form of the word-grouping strategy. You may wish to teach an entire group or class or individual pupils.

Jumble the sentences provided in Exhibit 7.2 (p. 130) or make up your own anagrams, using a vocabulary with which your pupils are familiar.

The activity is conducted over a period of several days.

Procedure

1. Model the word-grouping strategy.
   a. A sample anagram, such as *see weak helps the that people he,* can be used. Say aloud: "I first find an action word—*helps.* Then I ask a *wh* question: *Who* helps? *He* helps."
   b. "I find another action word—*see*—and ask the *wh* question: *Who* see? *People* see."
   c. "I order the units *people see* and *he helps.*"

---

[6] Phyllis A. Weaver, "Improving Reading Comprehension: Effect of Sentence Organization Instruction," *Reading Research Quarterly* 1, no. 15 (1979): 129–45.

Exhibit 7.1   Model of Sentence Anagram Word-grouping Strategy for Declarative Sentences in the Active Voice

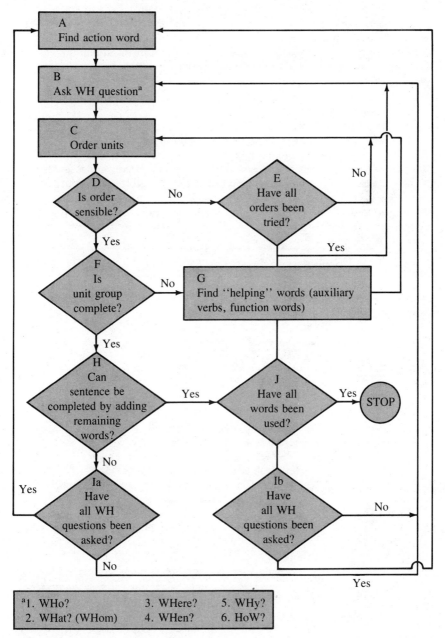

Source: Phyllis A. Weaver, "Improving Reading Comprehension: Effect of Sentence Organization Instruction," *Reading Research Quarterly* 1, no. 15 (1979): 137.

Activity 7.1   *(Continued)*

    d. "I check the words for meaning. *People see the weak* doesn't make sense. *He helps the weak* makes sense."

    e. "Can I add other words to complete the sentence? *People see that he helps the weak.*"

2. Ask pupils to imitate the above procedure in applying the strategy. Start with the jumbled sentence *owner ran him the after.* Perform all steps in this order:

    a. Find the action word.

    b. Ask *wh* questions.

    c. Order units.

    d. Ask, is the order sensible? If not try other orders.

    e. Complete the sentence by adding the remaining words.

3. Let pupils organize sentence anagrams derived from the sentences in Exhibit 7.2 or anagrams of your own construction. Start with sentences five to six words in length. Record time and encourage pupils to better their time. Move to anagrams of greater length when there are no errors.

Exhibit 7.2   Sentences to Jumble as Anagrams

Number of Words	Sentences
5–6	the happy boy found him
	your dog won't growl at friends
	let's eat in a little while
	the lion cut his paw
7–8	you can learn to earn money now
	the clock fell down from the wall
	she didn't want to kill the duck
	the fast ball was thrown by Andy
	the bird builds her nest in the water
9–10	the little cub ran home but the others didn't
	a bright light filled the room bringing cheer and hope
	you must scrub the wall before asking for any money
11–12	she saw that the dark cake baked giving off a sweet smell
	the tree came from a seed that had been brought from Spain
	does it help to plan before going on a long trip
13–15	the black and blue colors showed that something had happened before the circus left town
	dogs bark lions growl but only people brag and without a very good reason

You will note that the sentences in the panel call for comprehending passive voice, anaphora, and connectives.

SUMMARY

Comprehension depends upon recovering the meaning that underlies different kinds of sentences. The meanings of some sentences are more difficult to recover—those in passive form, those with relative clauses, those with reverse temporal ordering, and those with a semantic conflict. Strategies are presented for helping pupils unravel these difficult sentence structures.

Obviously the comprehension of a simple sentence depends upon the use of a wider context—successive sentences in the paragraph and even successive paragraphs in the text. A key factor in relating sentences within the paragraph is the ability to interpret anaphoric relationships. This chapter introduces some of the most commonly encountered anaphoric relationships and suggests strategies for helping readers resolve such relationships. The point is made that the deriving of antecedents for particular expressions not only depends upon form as it appears in the sentence but upon content. A young reader may be able to interpret pronouns or pro-sentences in beginning materials but not in advanced materials.

Strategies are given for teaching other aids to comprehending and relating sentences—typographical devices (such as connectives), analogies, and figures of speech. The practical activity of solving sentence anagrams is presented in detail as an illustration of a way to help learners integrate a number of sentence-processing abilities.

Useful Reading

Barnitz, John. "Developing Sentence Comprehension in Reading." *Language Arts* 56 (November/December 1979): 902–08.

Richer, M. "Reading Comprehension of Anaphoric Forms in Varying Linguistic Contexts." *Reading Research Quarterly* 12 (1976–1977): 145–65.

Shaw, Stanley, and Robert Schreiner. "The Effect of Sentence Manipulation on Subsequent Measures of Reading and Listening Comprehension." *Reading Research Quarterly* 17, no. 3 (1982): 339–53.

8 Comprehending Different Types of Discourse

TYPES OF DISCOURSE

COMPREHENDING NARRATIVE TEXT
Metalevel Schemata for Stories
Rhetorical Devices for Identifying the Author
Questions That Integrate Text
Strategies for Finding the Inner Sense of Narrative

COMPREHENDING EXPOSITORY TEXT
Using Pattern Guides
Restructuring Text
Summarizing
Identifying Rhetorical Structures

SUMMARY

Overview

Previous chapters have featured the active processes by which the learner ties informational content to prior knowledge and uses general strategies in comprehending text. This chapter focuses upon the ways the learner can examine the text itself for the logical structure of the material—its form as well as its content. Although meaning does not reside in the text alone, it is important for the reader to know how authors cue meaning and flag important statements. Indeed, a powerful tool is to know how to take the author's organizational plan and restructure it into a form that will give greater understanding.

Children are more successful in acquiring information from stories than from prose organized in other ways. Yet, much of the knowledge of greatest worth comes from interaction with texts having more formal structural properties than simple narrative. Sophisticated literature, exposition, and descriptive writing involve a variety of organizational forms. The purpose of this chapter is to attend to the most important of these and to suggest ways for helping pupils learn how to apply knowledge of the forms in comprehending.

TYPES OF DISCOURSE

William Brewer has an interesting classification scheme for illuminating the cognitive structures underlying different organizational forms.[1] This scheme is based on the prose of the traditional types of writing—narrative, exposition, and description. Each category in the scheme emphasizes a different intent on the part of the author—to inform, to entertain, to persuade, or to present an aesthetic experience.

As seen in Exhibit 8.1 (p. 134), Brewer refers to these purposes as *discourse force*. An underlying cognitive structure is hypothesized for each type. Descriptive discourse attempts to capture a perceptual scene. Since vision is the predominantly involved sense in this category, the cognitive structure is thought to be visual-spatial. In the case of narrative, a series of events in time are depicted and related through a causal or thematic chain. Thus, the underlying cognitive structure consists of temporally occurring events having a causal or thematic coherence. Expository discourse sets forth abstract logical processes. The underlying structure, therefore, features induction, classification, and comparison.

As you probably noticed, the notion of discourse force involves some problems. Some types of discourse can be designed to inform and entertain at the same time; and, of course, the classification system considers only the point of view of the author, who may not have the same intention as the reader. Nevertheless, by noting surface clues to the underlying structure, the reader may be able to anticipate the author's purpose and to adopt a reading strategy appropriate for the structure. The presence of location words—*near, above, behind*—may indicate spatial structure; words such as *thus* and *because* suggest logical structure; and choice of a particular vocabulary—colloquial or formal language—may indicate whether the author's purpose is to entertain or inform.

COMPREHENDING NARRATIVE TEXT

This chapter discusses ways of comprehending narrative text and then discusses expository text.

---

[1] William F. Brewer, "Literacy Theory, Rhetoric, and Stylistics: Implications for Psychology," in *Theoretical Issues in Reading Comprehension,* eds. R. Spiro, B. C. Bruce, and W. F. Brewer (Hillsdale, N.J.: Erlbaum, 1980), pp. 221–39.

Exhibit 8.1   A Psychological Classification of Written Discourse Types

Discourse (Underlying Structure)	Discourse Force			
	Inform	Entertain	Persuade	Literary-Aesthetic
Description (Space)	Technical description Botany Geography	Ordinary description	House advertisement	Poetic description
Narrative (Time-Events)	Newspaper story History Instructions Recipes Biography	Mystery novel Western novel Science fiction novel Fairy tale Short story Biography "Light" drama	"Message novel" Parable Fable Advertisement Drama	Literary novel Short story "Serious" drama
Exposition (Logic)	Scientific article Philosophy Abstract definition		Sermon Propaganda Editorial Advertisement Essay	

Source: Brewer, p. 225.

Metalevel Schemata for Stories

Do you know about "Story Maker" and "Textman"? They are language arts activities represented in microcomputer courseware created so children could gain a sense of what makes a story.[2]

In "Story Maker," children are presented with an inverted tree design with boxes called nodes connected by lines called branches; a path through the tree starts at the top node, goes to the next, and continues

[2] Andree Newman et al., "Story Maker" and "Textman" (Boston: Bolt, Beranack and Newman, Inc., 1981).

through connected nodes until it reaches the bottom of the inverted tree. Each path forms a complete story. Children choose a segment at each of the various levels, learning quickly that early choices have definite consequences. Computer graphics display the tree structure. Story segments already chosen appear in a color different from that of the tree, while the current set of choices blinks. With each set of options is a "make up your own" option, although the child can choose to work toward a goal generated by the computer. The goal serves to focus attention on the sequence of the story and to guide the user in making choices about events, characters, and final outcome. The child must continually assess new information, anticipate what might happen next, and decide upon the option that will most likely produce the desired outcomes.

Similarly, in "Textman" the child must keep in mind the audience and purpose of the selection as well as attend to paragraphs that precede and follow a missing paragraph. Choosing correct sentences depends upon comprehending the context. The player draws meaning from context, which in turn helps develop an understanding of the structural relations of sentences to paragraphs and paragraphs to the complete text.

"Story Maker" and "Textman" are of interest in their own right and because they illustrate how instruction in reading comprehension is being influenced by research on the overall structure of narrative.

In Chapter 1, you were introduced to story grammar. Story grammar specifies a set of rules for creating a story hierarchy. At the top of the hierarchy are the setting, including characters and location; the basic theme; a few key episodes in the plot; and a resolution of the problem that motivated the characters to action. At lower levels are the subplots—activities of the characters that are necessary in allowing higher-level events to happen.

Pupils who have schemata for stories (a knowledge of story grammar) comprehend and recall stories better than those without the schemata. Instruction in schematic aspects of narrative aids comprehension. Jill Whaley and Dixie Spiegel, for instance, directly taught story structure to a group of fourth-graders, who thereafter outscored a control group in comprehending stories.[3] Lessons typically consisted of (1) conducting an overview and review; (2) telling about and illustrating one story element (protagonist—reaction and goal, attempts to achieve the goal, outcome); (3) giving other examples of the element; (4) eliciting examples of the element from the children; and (5) having pupils participate in activities that reinforce the element taught.

---

[3] Jill F. Whaley and D. L. Spiegel, "Improving Children's Reading Comprehension Through Instruction in Schematic Aspects of Narratives" (Paper presented at the annual meeting of the American Educational Research Association, New York, March 1982).

Rhetorical Devices for Identifying the Author

In keeping with the view that reading first of all is an act of communication between reader and author, Bertram Bruce recommends teaching rhetorical devices by which pupils can identify the author in the narrative. He calls these devices "stories within stories."[4] Bruce refers to explicit *embedding,* such as in Washington Irving's *Rip Van Winkle,* in which an implied author introduces the text, supposedly written by a historian. Other forms of explicit embedding are drama, letters, and parts of books within a text.

A second device that creates a story within a story is *commentary* by the author: "I cannot draw you a picture of Peter and Benjamin because it was quite dark." When readers recognize commentary, they sense the implied author as a character.

Other rhetorical devices by which the author expresses himself or herself include *irony,* when an author says something naive or ridiculous and the putative author's position is satirized; the *unrecognized narrator,* where a character who narrates is not a participant in the story; and the *engaged author,* where the narration is in the first person and the defined storyteller is separate from the implied author. *Immersion* is a device by which the author puts the reader into the story, as happens in "you are the hero" type books. And there is the *in-effect narration,* in which we as readers see the world so much through the mind of one character that we feel that the character is telling the story.

Questions That Integrate Text

Isabel Beck and Margaret McKeown have found that many sets of questions in instructional materials appear to disrupt comprehension of the story. That is, the questions suggested in the teachers' manuals are not likely to help pupils organize and integrate text content.[5] On the contrary, the frequently recommended practice of asking questions at different taxonomic levels (literal, inferential, critical) is suspect. Instead, teachers should ask questions based on the logical organization of events and ideas of central importance to the story and their interrelationships—story grammar. Thus, the teacher has the pupils first decide upon the starting point of the story and then list in summary form the major events and ideas that constitute the plot and the links between events, or the gist of

---

[4] Bertram Bruce, "Stories Within Stories," *Language Arts* 58 (November/December 1981): 931–35.
[5] Isabel L. Beck and Margaret B. McKeown, "Developing Questions That Promote Comprehension of the Story Map," *Language Arts* 58 (November/December 1981): 913–17.

the story. Implied ideas that are part of the story but are not directly stated should be included. Asking questions that will elicit information matching the progression of ideas and events is the last step.

Harry Singer and Dan Donlan's schema-general questions for use in summarizing narrative appear to conform to Beck's and McKeown's recommendations.[6] These questions follow the organization of a story and suggest a way to synthesize story information and reconstruct it as a unit:

1. *The Leading Character*
   a. Who is the leading character?
   b. What action does the character initiate?
   c. What did you learn about the character from this action?
2. *The Goal*
   a. For what does the leading character appear to be striving?
   b. What did you learn about the character from the nature of the goal?
   c. What courses of action does the character take to reach the goal?
   d. What did you learn about the character from the courses of action taken?
3. *The Obstacle*
   a. What is the first (last) obstacle the character encounters?
   b. How does the character deal with it?
   c. How does the character alter the goal because of this obstacle?
   d. What does this tell you about the character?
4. *The Outcome*
   a. Does the character reach the original goal or a revised goal?
   b. If successful, what helped most?
      _____ Forces within the character's control.
      _____ Forces outside the character's control.
   c. If unsuccessful, what hindered the character most?
      _____ Forces within the character's control.
      _____ Forces outside the character's control.
      Name them.
5. *The Theme*
   What does the story basically show? A struggle with self, nature, other people?

A successful strategy for advanced readers to use in reading narrative has been documented by Alan Purves in his study of high-achieving read-

[6] Harry Singer and Dan Donlan, "Active Comprehension: Problem-Solving Schema with Question Generation for Comprehension of Complex Short Stories," *Reading Research Quarterly* 17 (1982): 166–87.

ers in New Zealand.[7] With this strategy, the reader gives detailed attention first to the form of the text and then to its content and affect:

* *Questions of Form*
  Is the story well written? Is it like any other story I know? How does the story build up? How is it organized? How is the way of telling the story related to what it is about? What metaphors, images, or references to things outside the story are used? Has the writer used words or sentences differently from the way people usually write?
* *Questions of Content*
  Is the story about important things? Is it a trivial or a serious work? Is there a lesson to be learned? Does the story tell one anything about people or ideas in general? How can we explain the way people behave in the story? Is there a hidden meaning? Is there one part that explains the whole? When was the story written? What is the historical background of the story and the writer? What happens? Is this a proper subject for a story?
* *Questions of Affect*
  Does the story succeed in getting me involved? What does it tell me about people I know? What is the writer's opinion or attitude toward the people in the story? Are any of the characters like people I know? What emotions does the story arouse in me?

Strategies for Finding the Inner Sense of Narrative

Comprehension of literary text—biographies, plays, short stories, novels—requires that the reader get away from the direct meaning of statements and move to an analysis of their inner sense. This is true not only for the interpretation of figurative expressions but in the reading of what appears to be a straightforward statement. Even a sentence like *The cab is here* may involve a deeper meaning, such as *How difficult it is to part from a friend*. It is possible to read a work superficially, identifying the progression of events, or to read it deeply, making inferences about the motives of characters and author. By way of example, Flora Lewis, foreign affairs correspondent for the *New York Times*, in reading Zbigniew Brzezinski's memoirs as national security adviser to President Carter, was sensitive to how Brzezinski revealed more than he intended.[8] Lewis believed Brzezinski's Polish background permeated his outlook and cited

---

[7] Alan C. Purves, *Achievement in Reading and Literature* (Wellington: New Zealand Council for Educational Research, 1979).
[8] Flora Lewis, "The Adviser's Advice," *New York Times Book Review,* April 17, 1983, pp. 3, 29.

statements from the memoirs that revealed how this heritage colored the security adviser's thinking on every issue:

a. In recounting his exhilaration at the signing of the treaty turning over the Panama Canal to Panama, he compared U.S. relations with Central America to Soviet domination of Eastern Europe.
b. He said that he, an immigrant, felt a (typically Polish) sense of outraged national honor during the Iranian hostage crisis that was not shared by others.
c. He displayed a deep dislike for Russia, although he was not particularly anticommunist (China's ideology or even Cuba's didn't bother him unduly).

Deeper meaning is dependent upon the schemata with which the reader interprets the text; hence the meanings derived are more varied than those grasped by logical relationships alone. Equally good readers viewing the same set of complex facts will be sensitive to different facets and will strike different emphases in their comments. The ability to read deeply is a reflection of the reader's emotional sensitivity, reading accuracy, and ability to make logical inferences.

The teaching of reading for inner meaning has been inadequately studied. Some direction has been given, however, in the process of literary analysis and the techniques used by actors wishing to convey an inner sense of a play. For example, pupils can be introduced to the variety of meanings in a given selection by reading the selection orally using different intonations and pauses. They will immediately note how the meaning of text changes even though not a single word is changed. Likewise, just as method actors never begin by studying the text of their role but by getting familiar with the images and motives of the characters they are to portray (deciding what the characters would do in specific situations), so pupils can be asked to first master the motives and images of the characters they will read about. Later, when reading the text, pupils will not be limited to the conveyed meanings but will instead be more open to the deeper meanings that lurk within the text.

COMPREHENDING EXPOSITORY TEXT

In expository writing there are predominant patterns that structure the presentation of information and ideas. The pattern in most textbooks is likely to be either cause and effect (showing how something occurs because of other factors); comparison and contrast (pointing out likenesses and differences among ideas and events); time order (putting facts and events into a sequence); problem and solution (stating a question and its answer); or simple listing (enumerating facts, events, and ideas).

Recognition of the author's organizational pattern helps in comprehension of exposition by enabling the reader to see the logical connections. Techniques for finding and using patterns are: using pattern guides, restructuring text, and summarizing. Each of these techniques aims at relating the concepts in the text to each other and serves to draw out generalizations rather than specifics.

Using Pattern Guides

A pattern guide is a device to help readers see relationships and distinguish important from less important ideas. Steps in preparing and using guides are:

1. Identify the key idea or generalization to be gained from reading the material.
2. Identify the predominant pattern used by the author in the material—cause and effect, comparison and contrast, or other.
3. Illustrate the pattern and tell the class how you identified it.
4. Make clear to the students that their task is to place relevant information from the text within the pattern. If, for example, you have identified a comparison and contrast pattern, pupils should know what is to be compared and contrasted (the central idea) and then look for information that can be used in making the comparison.
5. Provide the pattern guide, consisting of key concept or generalization, pattern to be used, and directions. The directions should indicate the kind of information to be placed within the pattern.

Exhibit 8.2 illustrates pattern guides. Notice how the pattern guides alert the reader to the appropriate relationship in the textbook. Numbers of pages where relevant information is to be found may also be given. Partially completed answers serve to model the responses desired. Modeling may be necessary when pattern guides are first introduced.

After students complete their reading and respond to the pattern guide, the class should discuss the concept and the organizational pattern. Students may suggest other patterns that would have been appropriate. As with other aspects of reading comprehension, there are surface clues to aid readers in recognizing organizational patterns. Some words signal a comparison and contrast pattern (*on the other hand, but, in contrast*); others, a cause and effect pattern (*consequently, since, therefore, as a result, hence*).

Pattern guides do more than help pupils comprehend particular selections. Continued use of the guides will develop learners' perception of organizational patterns, as well as the habit of looking for structure in text and connecting information in the text to important generalizations.

Exhibit 8.2   Pattern Guides

"Organizing the Forces of Labor"—Chapter 20[a]

Cause/Effect

In this section, look for cause-effect relationships in the situations mentioned below. Add the cause or effect in the proper column.

Cause	Effect
1.	1. Saving money was difficult or impossible for unskilled labor (p. 400).
2. Owners felt it was necessary to keep labor costs as low as possible (p. 400).	2.
3.	3. Only the boldest workers dared to defy management and join a labor organization (p. 400).
4. By 1800's wages of unskilled workers exceeded skilled artisans (p. 401).	4.
5.	5. The workingmen's parties supported Jackson after 1828 (pp. 402–3).

[a] Pattern guide created from Craft, Henry, and John Krout, *The Adventures of the American People* (Chicago: Rand, McNally, 1970).

"The United States Divided"—Chapter 14[b]

Contrast/Compare

Using pages 264–265, you will contrast and compare the repercussions in the South and the North to the Supreme Court's decision in the Dred Scott case.

the South		the North
1. (Hint: newspapers)	1.	
2. (Hint: Democratic Party)	2.	
3.	3.	
4.	4.	

[b] Pattern guide created from Craft and Krout, 1970.

"Sleep, Fatigue, and Rest"—Chapter 4[c]

Listing

This section of your textbook *lists* many causes of fatigue (pp. 96–97). Some of the causes are physical and some are mental. Fill in the causes under the appropriate heading.

I. Physical causes of fatigue
    A. short burst of intense effort
    B. rapid growth
    C. lack of important food
    D. pg. 96, par. 3
    E.
    F.
    G.
II. Mental causes of fatigue
    A. pg. 96, par. 1
    B.

[c] Pattern guide created from Miller, Benjamin F., et al., *Investigating Your Health* (Boston: Houghton Mifflin, 1971).

"Religious Change in Western Europe"—Unit 4, Chapter 3[d]

Time Order

A time line is an excellent way to see the sequence of events. As you read about the religious leaders (pp. 229–236), fill in the events on the time line below. Write what happened under the date.

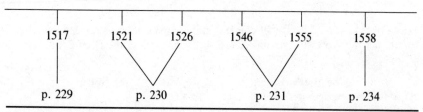

[d] Pattern guide created from Kownslar, Allan O., *People and Our World* (New York: Holt, Rinehart and Winston, 1977).
Source: Mary W. Olson and Bonnie Longnion, "Pattern Guides: A Workable Alternative for Content Teachers," *Journal of Reading* 25 (May 1982): 736–41.

Restructuring Text

The most common textbook organization is simple listing; the author makes a general statement and then supports it with a number of statements listed in no particular order. Words such as *also, moreover, and,* and *another* are surface indicators of a listing pattern. This pattern does not help the reader discern the more significant from the less significant ideas. It does not stress the relationships among key ideas.

A useful strategy for overcoming the disadvantages of listing is *restructuring*. Restructuring calls for taking a simple list and reorganizing it into a comparison and contrast pattern, a cause and effect pattern, or another pattern suggested by the content.

Donna Alvermann has found that using the restructuring strategy results in better comprehension of major points than merely following the author's listing.[9] In teaching a reconstruction strategy, Alvermann uses text material that contains randomly listed facts about a topic. This allows for a decision about a more useful pattern, such as cause and effect. A key term or organizer for the material is identified. A form is drawn that corresponds to the pattern selected. This form consists of empty boxes arranged to represent the slots into which information can be mentally inserted by readers as they process the material in their search for missing information.

After the teacher has modeled the restructuring technique, pupils are given an opportunity to construct their own organizers, using whatever patterns appear appropriate, to reconstruct passages from their textbooks.

[9] Donna E. Alvermann, "Restructuring Text Facilitates Written Recall of Main Ideas," *Journal of Reading* 25 (May 1982): 754–58.

Activity 8.1   Restructuring a Passage

Instructions

See if you can restructure the following passage on the topic of outlining, which is written in a listing pattern, by processing the passage as a comparison and contrast pattern. The key term in the passage is *forms for outlining.* This term suggests what is to be compared and contrasted. A response form, which includes the key term and empty boxes that represent slots for the contrasting ideas, has been provided in Exhibit 8.3. Read the passage, mentally filling in the empty slots.

Exhibit 8.3   Response Form for Restructuring a Passage on Outlining

Key term — *Forms for outlining*
Pattern — Comparison and contrast

Conventional outline	Array	Radial

After your own effort at reconstructing the passage, look at the sample restructuring appearing on page 146.

Passage to Restructure: Outlining

Outlining is used to help students clarify relationships. The conventional form for outlining is the familiar linear hierarchical ordering of ideas at different levels of subordination, with Roman numerals signaling the superordinate concepts; upper-case letters, the supporting or coordinate concepts; Arabic numbers, the subordinate details; and lower-case letters, the sub-subordinate details.

Another form is the *array*, a popular free-form outlining procedure whereby the student uses words, lines, and arrows as symbols to show the nature of the relationships. As indicated in Exhibit 8.4, an array reveals the reader's interpretation of text relationships.

Exhibit 8.4   An Array

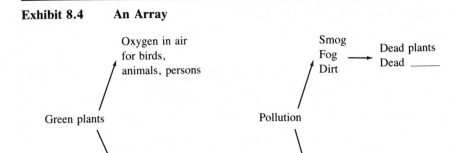

The correctness of an array depends upon the justification offered by the designer, with the information presented in the text and the inferences drawn taken into account. An array shows a spatial arrangement among key words and phrases. As indicated, it may also show sequence.

A third type of outline is the *radial,* another free form. The radial is used to distinguish superordinate from supporting or coordinate ideas, as shown in Exhibit 8.5. A disadvantage of the radial is that subordinate details are difficult to organize as a visual display.

Exhibit 8.5   A Radial

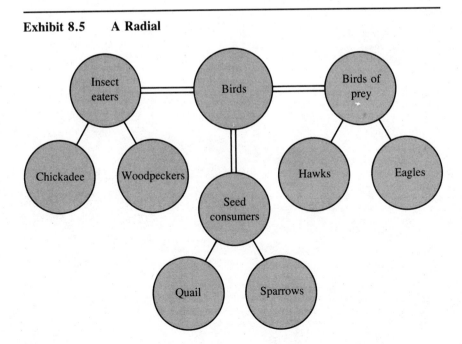

Exhibit 8.6   Sample Response for Restructuring a Passage on Outlining

Key term — *Forms for outlining*
Pattern — Comparison and contrast

Conventional outline	Array	Radial
Linear	Free form	Free form
Hierarchy of ideas	Interrelated ideas Sequence	Hierarchical relations
Roman numerals Upper-case letters Arabic numerals Lower-case letters	Words Lines Arrows	Words arranged in visual display

Summarizing

Making a summary is an important tool for understanding. It involves the basic operations for comprehending and remembering prose. In 1978 Walter Kintsch and Tuen Van Dijk published a model for comprehending text. This model specified the basic rules for processing text.[10]

Subsequently, after studying examples of children's and experts' successes in summarizing, Anne Brown and Jeanne Day identified six rules essential to summarization.[11] These rules are similar to the processing rules given by Kintsch and Van Dijk:

1. Delete unnecessary material—information that is trivial.
2. Delete material that is important but redundant.
3. Substitute a superordinate term for a list of items. If a text contains a list such as *chair, table, desk,* substitute the word *furniture.*
4. Substitute an encompassing action for a list of subcomponents of that action. For example: *John went to London* may be substituted for *John left the house. He went to the train station. He bought a ticket. . . .*
5. Select a topic sentence. The topic sentence, if there is one, usually is the author's summary of the paragraph.
6. If there is no topic sentence, invent your own.

Day trained junior-college students to apply the basic rules and to check to see that they were using the rules appropriately.[12] Prior to training, students deleted most of the unnecessary and redundant material but had difficulty in selecting topic sentences (only 25 percent did so accurately) and in inventing topic sentences (only 15 percent had success). Training in rule use—explicit instruction and modeling in the use of rules—was effective in general. Poorer students needed instruction in the control of the rules in order to maximize their performance. That is, they needed to be shown how to check that they had a topic sentence for each paragraph, that all redundancies were deleted, and the like. Application of the invention rule was difficult for most students and required the most explicit instruction and monitoring. The invention rule requires that students add information, producing something of their own, rather than merely deleting, selecting, and manipulating.

Note that the rules of summarization are general reading comprehension strategies involving operations essential in comprehending a wide

---

[10] W. Kintsch and T. A. Van Dijk, "Toward a Model of Text Comprehension and Production," *Psychological Review* 85, no. 5 (1978): 363–94.

[11] A. L. Brown and J. D. Day, "The Development of Rules for Summarizing Texts," (Unpublished manuscript, University of Illinois, 1980).

[12] J. D. Day, *Training Summarization Skills: A Comparison of Teaching Methods* (Doctoral dissertation, University of Illinois, 1980).

range of texts. Lisbeth Donant taught fifth-graders to apply the summarization strategy in reading unfamiliar passages. The reading comprehension of those so taught exceeded that of a comparable group of pupils.[13] In teaching the rules, Donant used materials two grade levels lower than the reading level of the pupils. The following paragraph illustrates materials used in helping pupils learn to find the topic sentence:

> The midnight rain stopped, leaving the house quite with only the echo of the dripping water. It was cold in the dark, empty building and the inspector shivered as he kept watch for the mysterious trespasser.
> a. A detective is staking out a house at night.
> b. Empty houses are scary at night.
> c. Someone is trespassing in the rain.

In teaching them to invent topic sentences, Donant had pupils listen to passages from selections in science, social studies, and literature. As the passages were read, pupils offered their own ideas about what the topic sentence should be, and these responses were discussed. Later, pupils invented topic sentences for paragraphs they read. Isolated practice of a rule was replaced with exercises demanding that all rules be applied in writing summaries for passages. The strategy training enabled pupils to excel both in summary writing and in the comprehension of fresh paragraphs. These results are consistent with those reported by Wittrock and others (Chapter 3), who found that elaboration by composition of summaries and headings greatly improved comprehension.

One caveat is in order. The rules for summary writing call for determining the relative importance of different parts of a text. What the reader thinks is important may not be what the author intended to be important. Someone reading for a particular purpose may judge relevancy differently from someone reading for another purpose. To the extent that pupils have shared goals, they should agree upon the parts of the text that form its gist.

Identifying Rhetorical Structures

Identifying and using the author's organizational framework are important in comprehending text. Pupils with this knowledge can relate the structure of the text to their own schemata, thereby learning what to expect from the text and how to process it. Bonnie Meyer, a specialist in the organization of text, has a classification system for identifying top-

---

[13] J. D. McNeil and L. Donant, "Summarization Strategy for Improving Reading Comprehension," *New Inquiries in Reading Research Instruction,* 31st Yearbook of the National Reading Conference, eds. J. Niles and L. Miller (Rochester, N.Y.: The National Reading Conference, 1982).

Activity 8.2   Applying the Summarization Strategy in the Study of Reading Comprehension

This activity has two purposes: (1) to give you the opportunity to validate the summarization strategy for yourself and (2) to help you think through a concern of many teachers of reading comprehension—how best to teach pupils to derive the main idea in text.

Instructions

First, read the following essay; then, write a summary sentence for each paragraph, applying as many summary-writing rules as are applicable. Finally, combine your summary statements into a summary of summaries (use format at end of essay). You should find that the procedure has a positive effect on your understanding of central ideas in text.

Essay to Be Read and Summarized

What is meant by *finding the main idea*? How should we teach pupils to do it? Let's start by looking at how comprehension tests define *finding the main idea*. Some require that the pupil choose the best title for a passage. Others ask that pupils identify the most general statement of three—for example: *The husky pulls the sled. Dogs work. The sheep dog watches the herd.* In some tests a brief story is presented along with several moral pronouncements, one of which might be inferred from the story. Other tests present a paragraph from which the pupil must select the factual generalization most consistent with the information in the paragraph. Occasionally, the pupil must identify or propose a theme that subsumes the ideas expressed in a number of paragraphs. Obviously, these tests are not measuring the same things. Identifying a topic sentence is much easier than inferring an unstated theme or generalization for a work.

Similar differences regarding the meaning of main ideas are found in writings on the subject. One writer says that any text can be divided into two, often unequal, parts. The first is the *theme,* or topic, of the text—the part that deals with what is already known. The second part, the *rheme,* is composed of new information about this subject. By this definition, topics are not main ideas, for they simply prepare the reader for what is to come. On the other hand, drawing conclusions from the new information is a main idea.

In contrast, another writer defines a theme as the main idea of a book, article, or chapter in a text. The theme may be implied or directly stated. If implied, the reader has to infer what the content of the text suggests about an aspect of the human condition or world knowledge. Still other writers say that the main idea of any piece is related to its location in the hierarchy of superordinate, coordinate, and subordinate terms. In a passage giving an example, a concept, and a generalization, the generalization must be the main idea.

Activity 8.2   (Continued)

Importance has something to do with main ideas. In fact, one author has proposed (facetiously) a test to rate the importance of main ideas. He calls it the *aha!—so what!* test.* If the main idea elicits an *aha!* reaction, it's probably a meaningful conclusion. If it elicits a *so what!* reaction, it is probably a relatively vacuous summary label. The problem is, there is not always general agreement among readers of all ages and places as to what is important. When readers are asked to read from given perspectives, they show greater agreement as to which ideas are important than when they read from their own perspectives.

Identifying main ideas in expository pieces is more difficult than in narrative. In narratives, importance means centrality to the story; character, goals, and setting are high in the hierarchy, and particular events are low. In expository texts, importance usually means how superordinate the idea is in a hierarchy leading from specific to general statements.

What does all this have to do with helping pupils recognize main ideas? For one thing, it means you have to be clear about what you mean by main ideas before preparing your lesson. Teaching strategies should match whatever variety of main idea is the target of instruction. If the goal is to recognize what part of a text is essential to the meaning, then the pupil must be taught the elements that, if changed or omitted, would result in a different meaning. If the goal is to determine the important idea, pupils must be taught to ask, "Important to what?" Importance of ideas depends upon context and perspective.

* P. David Pearson and Dale D. Johnson, *Teaching Reading Comprehension* (New York: Holt, Rinehart and Winston, 1978).

Exhibit 8.7   Inferring the Topic Sentence

	Supporting sentences	Plants make their own food.
		Herbivores eat plants.
	Inferred topic sentence	Predators eat herbivores.
		Infer a topic sentence.

Activity 8.2 *(Continued)*

When recognition and invention of topic sentences are the aims, pupils should be taught to differentiate among sentences that (a) tell what is to follow, (b) give brief definitions, (c) make statements to be explained, and (d) sum up the details of a passage. Also, it is helpful for pupils to know that sometimes they must infer the topic sentence from other sentences, as indicated in Exhibit 8.7.

The inferring of a topic sentence, a low-level definition of main idea, requires a general ability to reason. In Exhibit 8.7, one might have reasoned that an appropriate topic sentence would include the idea of food chain, cycle of events, or another generalization that relates the three sentences.

When the goal is to remember central ideas of textbooks, teach pupils to study textbook summaries rather than merely reread the original prose. When the goal is to recognize a hierarchy of ideas, then semantic mapping, outlining, and categorizing, whereby propositions are placed in logical relation to each other, are appropriate. Keep in mind, however, that there is no such thing as *the* main idea of any work. Readers with different backgrounds and purposes for reading will generate different main ideas from the same text.

Write your summary, using this format for checking summary writing:

Rules Applied		*Summary Sentences*
1.	Deleted unnecessary material. _____	1.
2.	Deleted redundancies. _____	2.
3.	Substituted superordinate term for list. _____	3.
4.	Substituted superordinate term for a number of actions. _____	4.
5.	Selected a topic sentence. _____	5.
6.	Invented a topic sentence. _____	6.
		Summary of Summaries

level structures in expository writing.[14] She and her associates have found beneficial effects in recall and comprehension from use of the system. In fact, one associate, B. J. Bartlett, taught ninth-graders the top-level structure and thereby enabled them to recall nearly twice as much information from their reading as students without instruction in the system.[15] Activity 8.3 provides practice in the recognition of these structures.

[14] Bonnie Meyer, *Prose Analysis: Purposes, Procedures, and Problems,* Research report no. 1 (Tempe: Department of Educational Psychology, College of Education, Arizona State University, June 1982).

[15] B. J. Bartlett, *Top Level Structure as an Organizational Strategy for Recall of Classroom Text* (Doctoral dissertation, Tempe: Arizona State University, 1978).

Activity 8.3   Identifying Top-Level Structures

Four top-level structures are featured in this activity: covariance, adversative, attribution, and response. In using the *covariance* structure, the author compares two equally weighted arguments regarding the cause of something: "Most wrecks result from a *lack of power* and a *lack of steering equipment* to handle emergency situations." An *adversative* structure compares a favored view with a less desirable opposing view: "In contrast to the ineffective remedy of offering more phonics for the poor reader, specialists recommend building background knowledge." The *attribution* structure describes the qualities associated with a person, event, or idea: "Trustworthy, kind, and reverent, Spike earned his merit badge." The *response* structure is found in question-answer and problem-solution formats: "How can we conserve energy in this house? We can insulate and look at the use of solar power."

In her teaching of these structures, Meyer uses entertaining advertisements for practice. Can you find adversative, attribution, and response structures in these advertising captions?[16]

1. Most wraps just wrap. Reynolds Wrap wraps, molds, and seals tightly.
2. Cover Girl Oil-Control Makeup: no shining, no streaking, no yellowing, no fading, no blotching, no caking.
3. Want a tough stain out? SHOUT it out!
4. This is where a wrinkle could start. (Picture shows area around eyes of lovely model.) This is what could stop it. (Picture shows Maybelline's Moisture Whip.)

Directions

Read each of the following passages—"Miracle Rice," "Anthrax," "Chicken-Hawks," and "How Historians View History." Identify the top-level structure in each passage. Check your responses with the answers at the end of the activity.

[16] Answers: (1) adversative, (2) attribution, (3) response, (4) response.

Activity 8.3   *(Continued)*

Miracle Rice*

There is a miracle rice that grows well in places in the Phillipines. And in West Africa, too. It is a miracle rice because it grows well where it is hard to grow anything at all. It grows fast. It produces big crops. It has the right color and taste. It contains large quantities of vitamins, particularly of the vitamin B family. These vitamins help people fight disease so that the rice is a good food. It is an easy crop to harvest and store. The rice is larger than other varieties and is bulkier. It can produce food for many, many people. So, it is a miracle rice.

Anthrax*

Scientists had puzzled for a long time about how animals got a disease called anthrax. It was a disease that was killing many cattle and other farm animals. It was also killing many wild animals, but it was the loss of stock that worried farmers, scientists, and the general public most of all. Sick animals had rod-like organisms in their blood. The animals gradually lost weight and strength and finally died. No one could understand why or how it happened. Finally, Robert Koch discovered the cause of anthrax. The disease was caused by a bacteria. Koch's discovery led to a treatment for anthrax.

Chicken-Hawks*

In one district, farmers began to kill the chicken-hawks. Large parties of men would go on bird-shoots. They not only shot adult birds, but also destroyed nests and breeding areas used by the hawks. Any young found in the nests were killed immediately. As a result of these hunts the farmers' chickens were not eaten. But, the farmers found something else wrong. Their store of grain in the barns was eaten by rats. Soon the rats were overrunning the farms. There was nothing to stop the spread of the rats. The farmers had removed a natural enemy of rats—the chicken-hawk.

How Historians View History**

Different views exist among historians on how history might be studied. These differences may be grouped into the view of history as a game,

* The three passages above were created from Morholdt, E., P. F. Brandwein, and L. S. Ward, *Biology: Patterns in the Environment* (New York: Harcourt Brace Jovanovich, 1972).
** This passage was created from Hyma, A., and M. Stanton, *Streams of Civilization* (San Diego: Creation Life Publishers, 1976).

Activity 8.3   *(Continued)*

and the view of history as a stream. Some historians view history as a game with players, rules, and clever plans. The players are people of all civilizations. The rules are the many sciences: such as biology, geology, archaeology, and geography. By studying people of the past and their planned "moves," we discover which moves lead to success or bring destruction. However, each person must first decide whether to be an active player in the game of history or a "pawn." As players, we try to improve the world in which we live. As pawns, we ignore the moves and decisions that others make which affect our lives.

Other historians see history as a stream. On the surface it appears to flow steadily onward, moving at will. Actually, however, it is slowed down, changed, and forced onward by strong undercurrents. This view is not as prominent as the other, but, no matter what their viewpoint, historians agree that history does repeat itself. Human nature and life today are not much different from the way they were in the days of Noah, Caesar, or Kennedy. Decisions facing us today are much the same as ones that had to be made in the past. History is the study of things that are past. It also helps us to understand what is happening in the world today, and it is a guide to what might be happening tomorrow.

Answers

"Miracle Rice." Most of the text is attribution, giving a collection of descriptions about the rice.
"Anthrax." This text is organized with a response problem-solution structure.
"Chicken-Hawks." This passage is organized with a covariance structure. Two conflicting ideas are presented. (If you noted that an antecedent-and-consequence structure is also used, you are correct.)
"How Historians View History." This passage contains an element of adversative structure: "This view is not as prominent as the other."

SUMMARY

This chapter introduces two types of discourse—narrative and exposition—and presents teaching strategies for helping readers comprehend both types. With respect to comprehending narrative, emphasis is given to understanding story grammar, identifying the author in the text, and asking questions that will integrate the events and ideas of central importance. In considering exposition, primary attention is given to the organizational patterns that structure the presentation of information and ideas. Strategies for teaching these patterns are: the pattern guide, restructuring techniques, summarization, and recognition of top-level rhetorical structures.

The teaching strategies associated with both narrative and exposition can contribute to a greater goal than enhanced comprehension of particular passages. They can become learning strategies that transfer to a wide range of material. This is true, at least, when the strategies are successfully modeled and practiced as well as when there is a conscious recognition by readers of how the strategies can help them derive meaning from text.

Useful Reading

D'Angelo, F. J. "The Search for Intelligible Structure in the Teaching of Composition." *College Composition and Communication* 27 (1976): 142–47.

McConkie, G. W. "Learning from Text." In *Review of Research on Education*, ed. L. Schulman (Itasca, Ill.: F. E. Peacock, 1977), pp. 3–48.

Mandler, J. M., and N. S. Johnson. "Remembrance of Things Parsed: Story Structure and Recall." *Cognitive Psychology* 9 (1977): 111–51.

Coda

This concluding portion is but one possible summary for the text. You may prefer to write your own. The purpose of the coda is twofold: (1) to reiterate the major assumption and accompanying hypotheses about reading comprehension and (2) to place the featured teaching and learning strategies within a utilization-related framework.

Throughout the book there is an underlying assumption that meaning of text is not only found in printed material but is discovered and created through interaction between reader and text. Consistent with this assumption are four associated hypotheses:

1. The *prior-knowledge hypothesis,* which holds that what one knows determines what one will learn.
2. The *importance-of-both-concept-and-text hypothesis,* which holds that both one's schemata and attendance to textual features are necessary for determining meaning from reading.
3. The *deep-processing hypothesis,* which holds that the deeper one processes text—both by elaborating (drawing inferences) and by relating the ideas in text to each other through the use of organizational patterns and summarization strategies—the more the text will be remembered.
4. The *importance-of-context hypothesis,* which holds that the perspective from which one reads influences the meaning derived.

Although the underlying assumption and hypotheses may appear commonplace, much current practice indicates otherwise. The use of readability formulas that purport to assess difficulty on the basis of text variables alone—without regard to the reader's familiarity with and interest in the content—is a case in point. The prevailing practice of assessing and teaching comprehension by presenting a brief passage followed by multiple choices—only one of which is presumed to be *the* correct meaning—belies a constructivist hypothesis. Other practices that are inconsistent with the interactive view of reading include use of lesson plans that feature teacher-initiated questions to the exclusion of pupil-initiated questions, failure to find out what in the learner's background is relevant to the material to be read, and failure to help the reader learn how to connect prior experiences with the text at hand. Please note that determining whether a learner has particular knowledge about a topic as a means for assessing readiness for reading is not the same as taking whatever the learner knows and using it as a bridge to the new material. In too many classrooms pupils are asked to find main ideas, to draw conclusions, and to determine cause and effect relations without instruction in how to achieve these tasks. Usually the remedy prescribed for failure is more of the same—testing rather than teaching. In contrast, I believe that the interactive teaching and learning strategies described in this book offer a new direction to classroom practice.

As seen in the utilization-related framework presented in Exhibit C.1, the decisions, content, and strategies for instruction tend to be sequential—to occur before, during, and after reading. This is not to say that any reading strategy is restricted to a particular phase. The posing of questions, for example, is more frequent in the initial phase but can occur at any time during the reading process. The factors and procedures involved in reading narrative often differ from the strategies used in reading exposition. Once the choice has been made to read narrative, certain strategies loom in importance. A schema for story grammar, for instance, is activated in setting reading expectations for narrative. In contrast, after choosing to read exposition, the reader must activate a schema relevant to the subject at hand.

The abbreviated questions in the diamond-shaped squares in Exhibit C.1 signify important questions a teacher should ask about the prerequisite competencies of students for engaging in the reading comprehension process. For example, before having them read exposition, the teacher should know what hierarchical associations pupils already have with respect to the topic featured in the text.

The headings in the boxes indicate the strategy, which should be either to gain necessary information about the learner or to help the learner acquire the strategy for independent reading. For example, after pupils have read a story, it is important to know what personal meaning they derived from the narrative; so the teacher might have them engage in story retelling. Story retelling, however, is also a good technique for remembering a learning strategy to be acquired.

The flow-chart has several functions. You can use it to check your own conceptual framework of the teaching-learning process of reading comprehension. Are there omissions or deletions you wish to make? You can add key factors and procedures in the spaces provided. It is likely that experienced teachers have ideas that will enhance the framework. Further, as new knowledge of the comprehension process is attained, the framework can be augmented and revised.

You may use the framework together with the book to verify your understanding of the strategies. If, for instance, you are unsure about semantic mapping, self-interrogation, or another strategy, reread the appropriate sections. You will note that each of the boxes in the chart is coded with a number. The numbers refer to sections in the book, as specified in the list at the end of Exhibit C.1 (p. 165). Explanations and illustrations for the strategies are found in these sections.

The framework also can serve as a basis for group discussion. You and your colleagues will gain something by questioning the sequencing or placement of certain procedures. By way of example, consider whether the use of typographical aids in narrative differs from their use in exposition. Admittedly, the comma, period, and other marks signal meanings that are common to both types. But are there not differences as well? In narrative, italics may signal irony; while in exposition, italics are more likely to indicate foreign terms or to stress a certain point. Similar questioning of the different applications of debugging, revising, and other strategies in relation to types of reading is in order.

I hope you will find a way to integrate aspects of the framework into your own thinking about reading comprehension. In addition to helping you to recall the strategies and to think about when to apply them in your teaching, the framework can serve another purpose: ask yourself, "How does the framework—the ideas represented by it—affect the way I perceive and judge the teaching and learning of reading comprehension?"

Exhibit C.1   Flowchart for Reading Comprehension

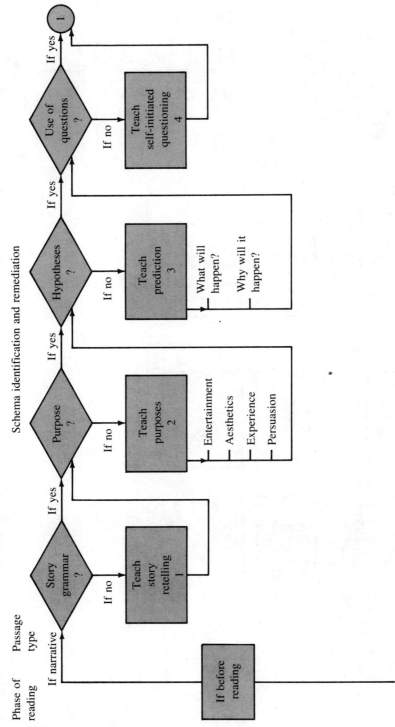

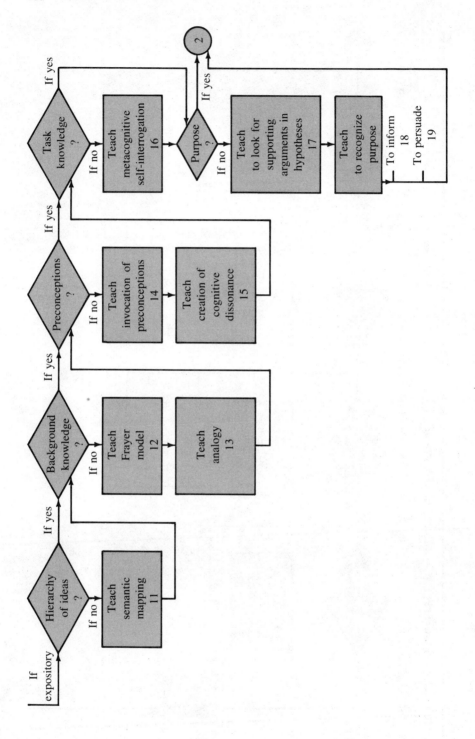

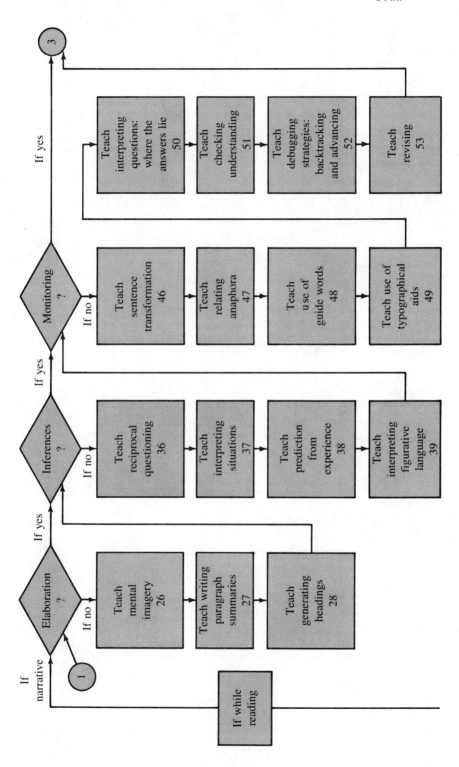

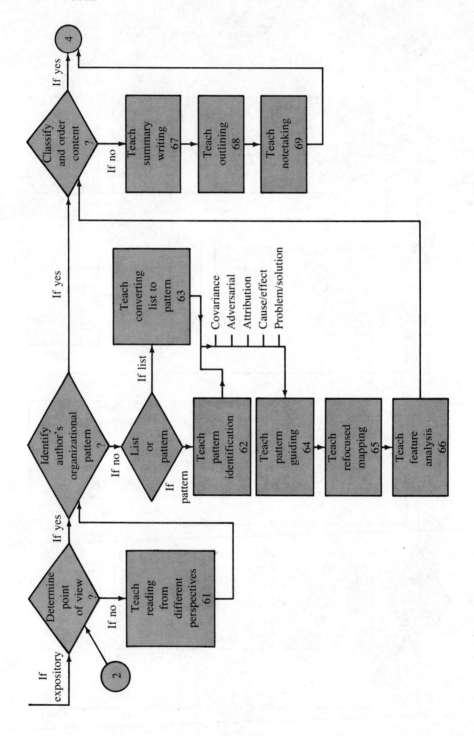

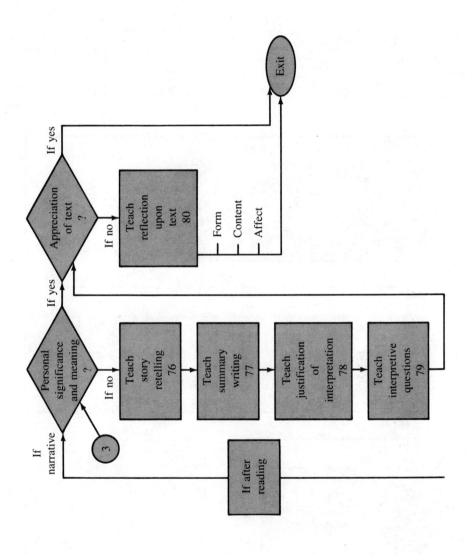

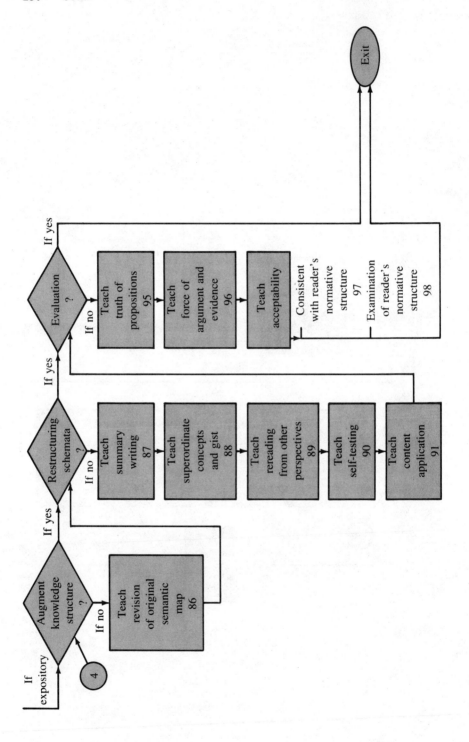

Teaching and Learning Strategy	Textbook Reference
1. Story retelling	
2. Purpose for narrative	
3. Making predictions	
4. Self-initiated questioning	
5. [a]	
6.	
7.	
8.	
9.	
10.	
11. Semantic mapping	
12. Frayer model	
13. Analogy	
14. Invocation of preconceptions	
15. Cognitive dissonance	
16. Metacognitive self-interrogation	
17. Looking for supporting arguments	
18. Informing	
19. Persuading	
20.	
21.	
22.	
23.	
24.	
25.	
26. Mental imagery	
27. Paragraph headings	
28. Generating headings	
29.	
30.	
31.	
32.	
33.	
34.	
35.	
36. Reciprocal questioning	
37. Interpreting situations	
38. Predicting	

[a] Use the blanks to make your own additions to the framework.

Teaching and Learning Strategy   Textbook Reference

39. Interpreting figurative language
40.
41.
42.
43.
44.
45.
46. Sentence transformations
47. Anaphora
48. Guide words
49. Typographical aids
50. Interpreting questions
51. Checking comprehension
52. Debugging
53. Revising
54.
55.
56.
57.
58.
59.
60.
61. Reading from different perspectives
62. Pattern identification
63. Converting list to pattern
64. Pattern guides
65. Refocused mapping
66. Feature analysis
67. Summary writing
68. Outlining
69. Notetaking
70.
71.
72.
73.
74.
75.
76. Story retelling
77. Summary writing
78. Justifying interpretation

Teaching and Learning Strategy	Textbook Reference
79. Intepretive questioning	
80. Reflecting upon text	
81.	
82.	
83.	
84.	
85.	
86. Revising semantic map	
87. Summary writing	
88. Superordinate concepts and gist	
89. Reading from other perspectives	
90. Self-testing	
91. Content application	
92.	
93.	
94.	
95. Truth of propositions	
96. Force of argument and evidence	
97. Acceptability to normative structure	
98. Examination of normative structure	

Index